AMAZING RUBBER BAND CARS

Easy-to-Build Wind-Up Racers, Models, and Toys

Mike Rigsby

CHICAGO
REVIEW
PRESS

Library of Congress Cataloging-in-Publication Data

Rigsby, Mike.

    Amazing rubber band cars : easy-to-build wind-up racers, models, and toys / Mike Rigsby.
      p. cm.
    ISBN-13: 978-1-55652-736-4
    ISBN-10: 1-55652-736-5

1. Automobiles—Models—Juvenile literature. 2. Toys—Juvenile literature. 3. Paperboard—Juvenile literature. I. Title.

    TL237.R54 2007
    629.22'18—dc22

2007013969

Cover design: Scott Rattray
Cover photographs: Mike Rigsby and StockByte
Interior design: Scott Rattray
Photo credits: Mike Rigsby

© 2008 by Mike Rigsby
All rights reserved
Published by Chicago Review Press, Incorporated
814 North Franklin Street
Chicago, Illinois 60610
ISBN-13: 978-1-55652-736-4
ISBN-10: 1-55652-736-5
Printed in the United States of America
5 4

To my parents, Conrad and Kathryn

Acknowledgments

I would like to thank my wife, Annelle, for tolerating cardboard cars zipping around the house. Thanks to our daughters, Tia and Ember, for drawing assistance and encouragement.

I can't omit the tireless efforts of my agent, Renee Zuckerbrot, as well as the assistance of my editor, Jerome Pohlen. Last, I won't forget the ladies at work who smiled and patiently nodded affirmation every time I showed off my latest and most fantastic cardboard creation.

Contents

Introduction

The cars and toys in this book are designed to be easily assembled from common household materials. Construction of a car requires only cardboard, glue, pencils, and rubber bands. My hope is that parents will build these cardboard cars with their kids. You can work together, build memories, and share a book. Whether you plant the seeds for a future engineer or retain a lifetime memory of cardboard glued to the carpet, something significant will happen.

By spending time with their children, parents can open the lines of communication. If you ask a child how things went at school, the answer will probably be "Fine." But if you're working through this book together, the stories about friends, bullies, and teachers will emerge.

Engineering is the application of scientific principles (knowledge) to practical things that people use. Applying knowledge from this book to household materials will produce practical things (toys) for kids to use. Although there is no mention of Newton's third law, or "translation of linear motion to rotational motion," the child who is fascinated by this book has interests that may lead to a future career in the sciences. Parents should support their child's interests by exposing them to different ideas. This book is appropriate for the child who is interested in moving objects and building things. It is also appropriate for the child who has never been exposed to engineering concepts.

For the child who isn't interested in books, *Amazing Rubber Band Cars* has plenty of pictures, not too many words, and a practical spin—read it and learn how to build toys. It will spark a child's interest in reading.

Building toys from scratch may inspire a future engineer. It may help the future pastry chef to make gingerbread houses. But the most important outcome may just be a memory such as "Remember when we made those rubber band cars together?"

Note to Builders

Ａll of the cars in this book are built with corrugated cardboard. Corrugated cardboard is a thick "board" made of an arched layer between two smooth sheets. You can tell if cardboard is corrugated by looking at its edge.

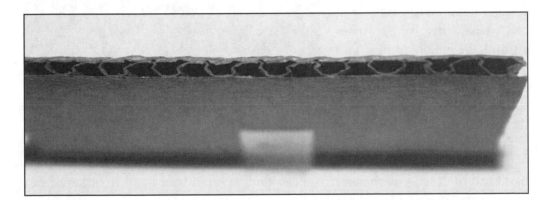

Corrugated cardboard is a good construction material for several reasons. It is stiff enough to make parts that will resist bending. Parts can be cut easily using scissors, and holes can be punched using a push pin or pencil point. Corrugated cardboard works well with white glue, and it makes for solid assemblies. And if you rescue old boxes from the trash, the cardboard costs nothing and you are recycling, which is good for the environment.

Flat cardboard, the kind you find used for a cereal box, will work for the basic car, but you will spend quite a bit of time holding flat pieces together waiting for glue to dry. Thick or solid cardboard makes nice parts but is difficult to cut with scissors. That doesn't mean you can't use these materials. You should think of this book as a guide, a starting point. When you see how your car works, try using different materials and modify the designs to make them your own.

When gluing corrugated cardboard, most pieces will stay together after about 30 seconds of holding them with your fingers. White glue needs about 30 minutes to dry completely; if you don't wait long enough, your pieces may pop apart when you stretch the rubber bands. If you don't want to wait 30 minutes, give it a try earlier. If anything fails, you can always glue parts back together or make another piece.

Save your templates from all the projects in a large envelope so that they will not be damaged or lost when you want to build again. Each template has been given a code to help you keep them straight.

The plans in this book attach the rubber band to the axle. This keeps the rubber band with the car, but it causes the wheels to stop turning as soon as the rubber band unwinds. To 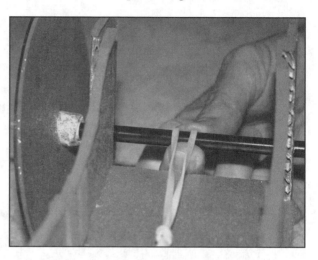 maximize the distance that a car will travel, the rubber band needs to release from the axle when its work is done, thus allowing the car to coast ahead. If you'd like to modify the design, instead of attaching the rubber band to the axle, you can wind the rubber band around the axle each time you wind the car. An easy way to accomplish this is to hold the rubber band to the axle while the first turn is made. Friction will hold the rubber band while you continue to wind the car. The rubber band will release when the axle unwinds.

Rubber bands come in different sizes and colors. I used 3½-inch by ⅛-inch bands on my cars. Use whatever you can find. If the rubber band stretches, it can be used to move the car. Experiment!

The Basic Rubber Band Car

In this chapter you will learn will learn how to build a basic cardboard car powered by rubber bands.

Materials and Tools

$\frac{1}{8}$-inch-thick corrugated cardboard
Scissors
Pushpin
2 round pencils

White glue
2 rubber bands
D-cell battery

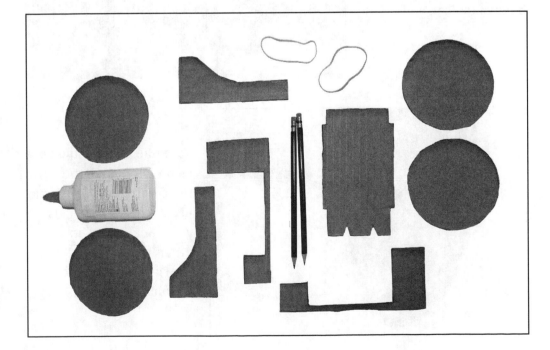

Time to get started. Copy the templates from pages 11 and 12 onto cardboard. You will need one **Floor** (1A), two **Frames** (1B), two **Side Rails** (1C), and four **Wheels** (1D). Cut all the pieces from a section of corrugated cardboard. Take care to make the wheels as round as possible. Use the pushpin to mark the center point of the holes for the pencils on the two frame pieces.

The wheels and the frame need axle holes. While you could use a hole punch to create these in the frame, no ordinary hole punch will reach to the center of the wheels. Instead, take a pushpin and insert it into the center point of the wheel. Then remove the pushpin and insert a pencil.

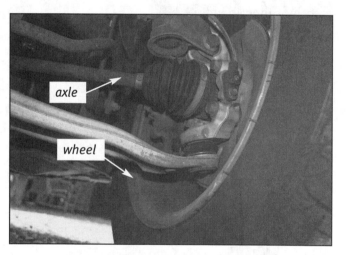

Each pencil on your cardboard car works like the axle on a real car. A car's axle allows the wheel to turn without spinning the body of the car.

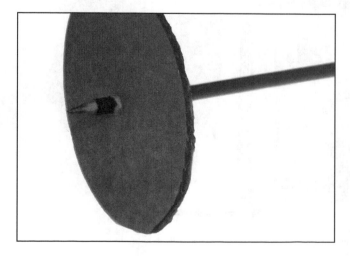

Continue pushing the pencil until it passes through the cardboard. When making the holes in wheels, you want a snug fit. In other words, when the pencil turns, the wheel should turn as well.

Now make the axle holes in the frame pieces. It is best if the holes are big and loose, since the pencils need to turn freely in the frame—when the axles turn, the frame should *not* turn. Move the pencil left, right, up, and down to make the axle holes in the frames bigger.

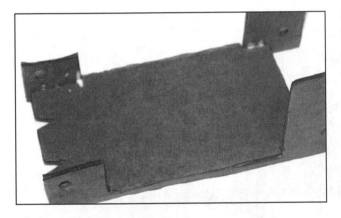

Glue the floor to the two frame pieces. Place glue wherever cardboard touches cardboard.

Next, glue the side rails to the frame. The side rails go *inside* the frame on both sides.

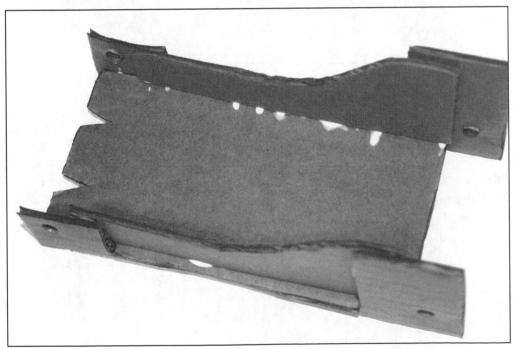

It's time to attach the wheels to the axles. Push one of the wheels over a pencil and slide it close to the eraser end. Place glue around the pencil close to the eraser, then slide the wheel over the glue.

Insert the wheel and pencil through the axle holes at the back of the car frame. (The back is the high part of the frame.)

Push a second wheel onto the other end of the pencil and glue it into place.

Now assemble the front wheel and axles. Push a wheel onto the second pencil, glue it, and then insert the pencil through the frame's front axle holes. Add the final wheel onto the other end of the pencil and glue it in place.

Once the glue has dried, you are ready to attach the rubber bands to the axle. This is a simple process, and it is explained below, step by step.

First, place one rubber band under the rear pencil. Tab A in the photo has been placed on one end of the band to make things clearer. (You won't need it on your rubber band, though.)

Now pull the Tab A end of the rubber band over the top of the pencil and down through the other end of the band, as shown.

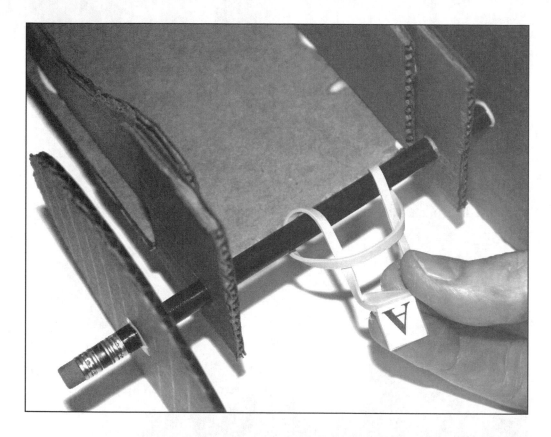

Pull the Tab A end of the rubber band up over the pencil and lay it on the floor of the car.

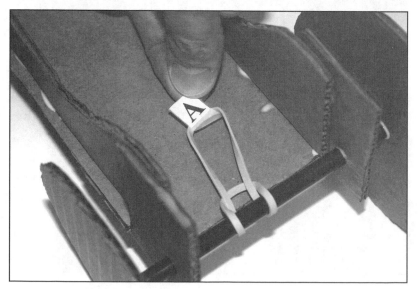

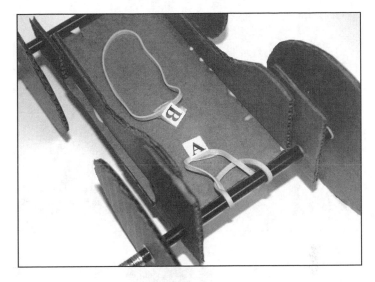

The rubber band with Tab A is lying at the back of the car. Place a second rubber band, labeled with Tab B here, on the floor of the car.

Move the second rubber band so that it is *under* the first rubber band, then pull the Tab B end through the first rubber band.

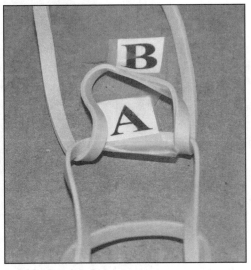

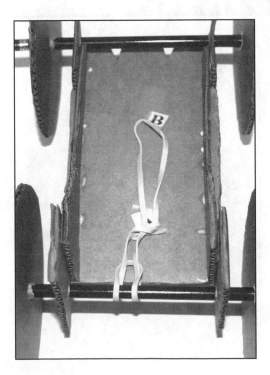

Pull the Tab B end through the forward end of the second rubber band until the two rubber bands are tightly linked together.

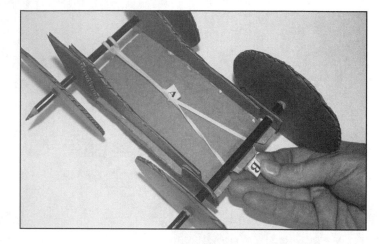

Stretch Tab B toward the front of the car. Loop Tab B over the two V-shaped slits at the front of the car.

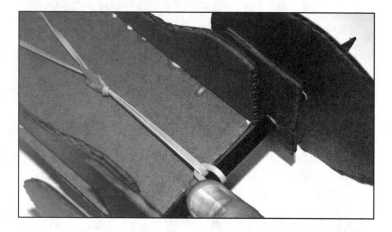

You are ready for a test run. Wind the rear wheel backward. If the rubber band slips, grasp it with your fingers until it wraps around the pencil one time.

Friction—the force between the wheel and the ground—is necessary for the car to move. Without friction, the wheels will turn like tires on ice, and your car will not move. And, once the car is moving, friction is the force that causes the car to stop.

To increase the amount of friction, you can add weight to the car. Place a flashlight battery near the back axle, on the car's floor. If you race your car on a carpeted floor, you may not need a battery because the friction between the wheels and carpet is greater than the friction between the wheels and a smooth floor.

Try your racer again, with the battery for weight. Wind up the rubber band by turning the pencil axle backward, as shown. With the car on the ground, release the pencil and the car will move.

Decorating the Car

Now that you have built your car, it's time to decorate it. What follows is one idea, but you can probably come up with your own design. Be creative!

Materials and Tools

Yellow and blue acrylic paint
Paintbrushes
Water
Pistachio nut half shells

Scissors
Red craft foam
White glue

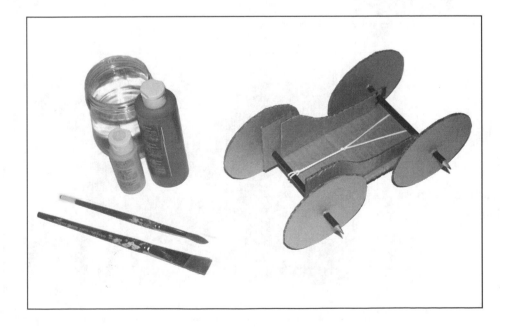

Start by painting the wheels of the car yellow. Paint the body blue. Use water to clean the brushes.

Take a brush and paint the empty half shells of pistachio nuts blue. When they are dry, you can glue them to the wheels. Cut red craft foam in any shape you want and glue it to the body and wheels.

Your racer is now finished!

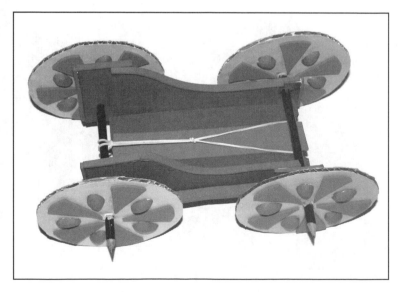

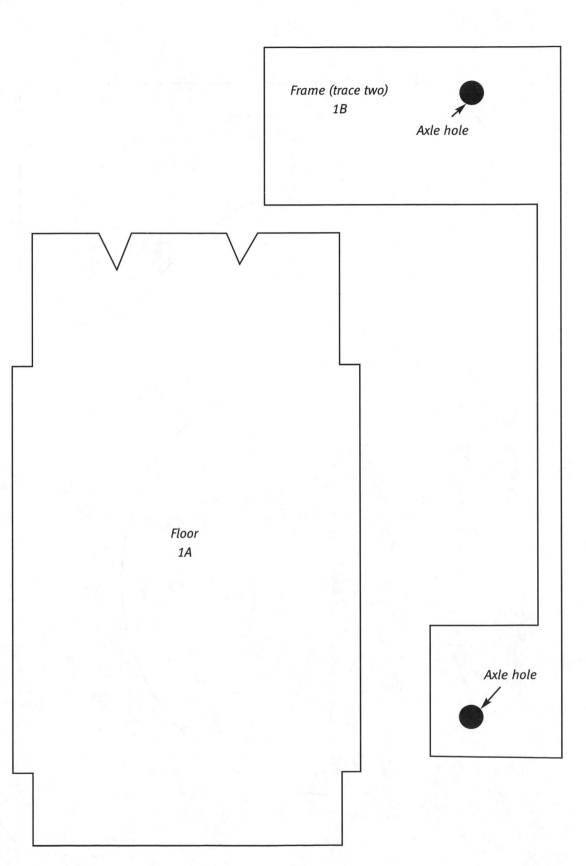

Frame (trace two)
1B

Axle hole

Axle hole

Floor
1A

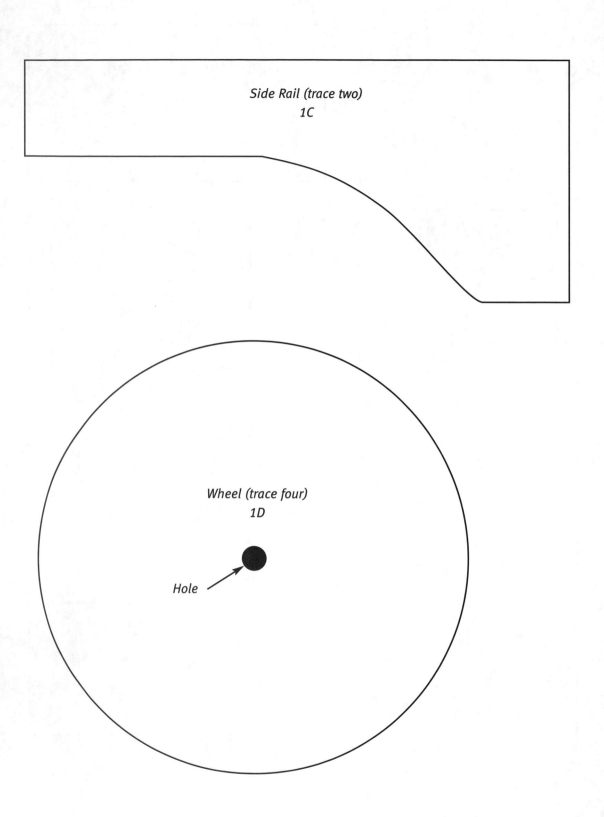

Side Rail (trace two)
1C

Wheel (trace four)
1D

Hole

Creative Wheels

Maybe you want to try using something different for wheels, like old compact discs (CDs). Here's a modification you can make to the Basic Rubber Band Car from chapter 1.

Materials and Tools

4 old compact discs
2 round pencils
Masking tape
2 rubber bands

Start by mounting a compact disc to one end a pencil. Wrap masking tape around the pencil (near the eraser end).

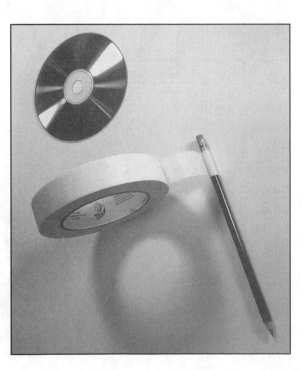

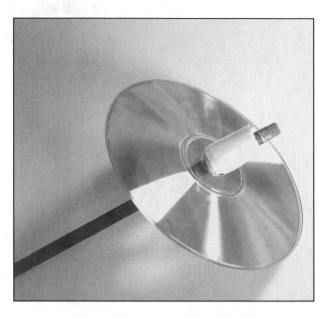

Continue wrapping until the combination of tape and pencil is slightly larger than the hole in the CD.

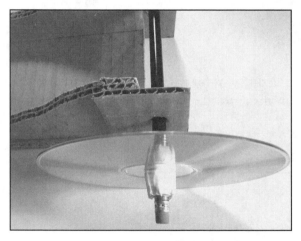

Push the CD onto the tape—it needs to be a tight fit. Insert the pencil axle through the back axle holes in the car frame.

Repeat the tape-wrapping process at the other end of the pencil. Mount a CD on the tape to complete the rear wheels and axle.

Repeat the process on the front of the car with another pencil and two CDs.

Attach the rubber bands to the rear axle using the same method in chapter 1. You're ready to go!

Decorating the Car

Materials and Tools

Paintbrush	Blue craft foam
Water	Scissors
Silver acrylic paint	White glue

To decorate this car, use a brush to paint the body silver. Clean the brush with water.

Using blue craft foam, scissors, and glue, add stripes and trim to decorate the car. Here's an example of the decorations on a finished racer.

Bearings and Friction

To make a car roll more easily, you must reduce the friction between the bearings and the axles. Bearings are the part of a machine in which an axle turns. The bearings on your car have been nothing more than a hole in a piece of cardboard . . . until now. You can reduce friction with a simple aluminum foil bearing.

Materials and Tools

Scissors
Ruler
Aluminum foil
2 round pencils

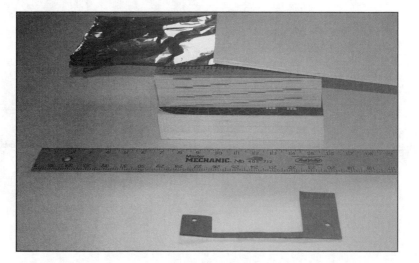

Start with the cardboard car frame from chapter 1. Insert the scissors into the axle holes and rotate left and right to enlarge each until both are about $\frac{1}{2}$ inch across.

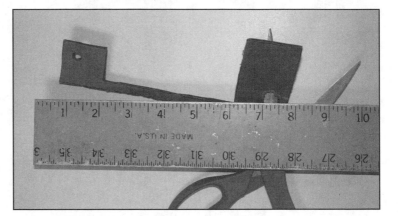

Take a piece of aluminum foil, about the size of a sheet of notebook paper, and fold it lengthwise, over and over in layers, into a strip that is about 1 inch wide.

The completed strip should look like the photo here.

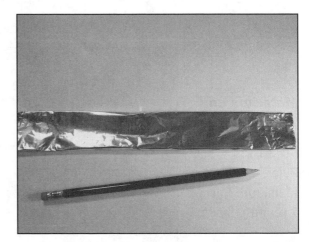

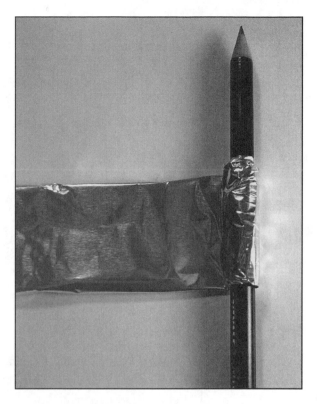

Wrap the folded foil strip around a round pencil.

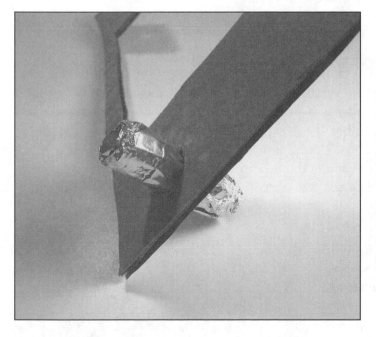

Insert the pencil with the foil tube into the cardboard frame. Depending on how large you made the hole with the scissors, it may be necessary to remove some layers of the foil, but the foil should fit snugly. Then remove the pencil.

Repeat the process for the other three frame holes and install the pencil axles and wheels.

Testing the Bearings

Compare your new and improved car with the basic cardboard car from chapter 1. Place the cars side by side on a "hill" made by placing books under one end a piece of foamboard or cardboard to create a slope. (Be sure to remove the rubber band from the basic cardboard car. Because you are testing the cars to see which one rolls more easily, neither car should have a rubber band or battery.) Slowly raise the board until one of the cars starts to roll.

The car with the aluminum foil bearings should roll down the hill first, while the car from chapter 1 (without the bearings) just sits there. Aluminum foil bearings make the car roll more easily than a car without bearings. To make the basic rubber band car roll, raise the foamboard. Raising the foamboard at

an angle causes the car to react in two ways. First, the force of gravity still wants to pull the car downward, toward the foamboard. When the foamboard was flat, it pushed back up with the same force, and the car sat still. But at an angle, the foamboard pushes back on the car in a slightly forward direction. Gravity pulls down while the foamboard pushes forward, and the car moves. Low forward force (board lifted a little) is needed

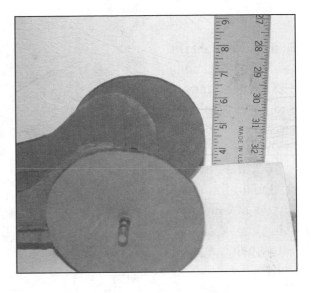

to overcome low friction (car with aluminum foil bearings). Higher forward force (board lifted high) is needed to overcome high friction (basic cardboard car).

Decorating the Car

Materials and Tools

Red and yellow
    acrylic paint
Glitter paint
Paintbrushes
Water
Thin ribbon
Scissors
Aluminum foil
White glue
Posterboard
Hole punch

First, if you want the car to be operational, add rubber bands and battery, following the instructions in chapter 1.

Decorate the cardboard frame and wheels of your car using acrylic paint, glitter paint, and ribbon.

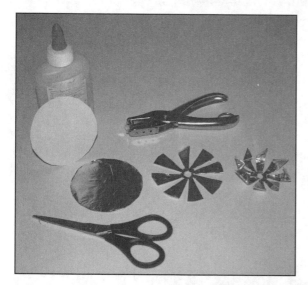

To make the foil spinners, cut circles—any size you like—from aluminum foil and glue them to circles cut from posterboard. Cut slots, punch a hole in the center of the circles, and bend each spinner into an interesting design.

Glue the spinners to the pencil axles to finish the decoration.

4

Distance Car

In this chapter, you will build a car that is designed to travel farther than the basic car. To make this happen, the rubber bands turn a pulley and this pulley turns an axle. Each turn of the pulley turns the axle several times, making the wheels turn more revolutions than on the basic car.

You may think this is magic—make a big enough pulley and the car will run forever—but there are limits. Bigger pulleys are harder for the rubber band to turn. If the pulley is too large, the rubber band won't be able to turn it, and the car will not move.

Materials and Tools

⅛-inch-thick corru-
      gated cardboard
Scissors
Pushpin
White glue
Hole punch
3 round pencils
1-foot length fishing
      line
2 rubber bands

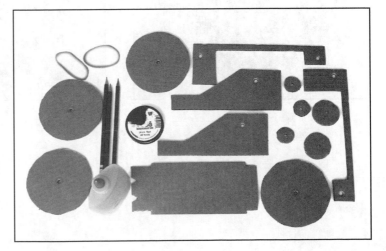

Copy the templates from pages 29, 30, and 31 onto cardboard. You will need four **Wheels** (4A), three **Inner Pulleys** (4B), two **Outer Pulleys** (4C), one **Floor** (4D), two **Frames** (4E), and two **Side Rails** (4F). Construct the basic car just as you did in chapter 1. The

car should look like the photo above. Notice that there are two new holes at the top of the side rails. You will use these holes to mount the pulley.

Glue the three small inner pulleys pieces together, making sure the holes align. Then glue the two outer pulleys to the inner pulleys. Finally, punch a hole into one of the outer pulley wheels, as shown.

Insert a pencil through one side rail hole. Add a spot of glue to the pencil, and slide it through the pulley wheels. Slide the end of the pencil through the other side rail hole.

Your car should now look like this.

Take one end of a 1-foot length of fishing line and insert it through the hole in the pulley wheel. Loop the line over the top of the pulley wheel and tie a knot at the point where the line first entered the hole.

Wrap the fishing line around the pulley, in the groove between the outer wheels, 7 times. Then take the other end of the fishing line to the rear axle and tie a tight knot around the pencil.

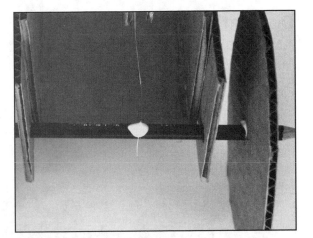

Place glue on the fishing line at the rear axle and let it dry completely.

Attach rubber bands to the pulley's axle, just as you did with the basic car. Your finished Distance Car should look like this.

To wind the car, slowly turn the rear axle. The pulley should turn along with the rear axle. As the pulley turns, be sure that the rubber band is turning—sometimes you have to use your fingers to keep the rubber band from slipping on the first rotation. When fully wound, at the point where the fishing line is wrapped around the rear axle, this car will travel at least three times as far as the Basic Rubber Band Car.

Decorating the Car

Materials and Tools

Light and dark blue acrylic paint
Ocean-themed stickers
Wiggle eyes
Paintbrushes

Water
White glue
Scissors

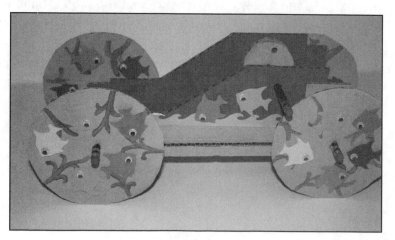

Here is just one idea for decorating your Distance Car—a fish in the ocean theme. Here's a finished car.

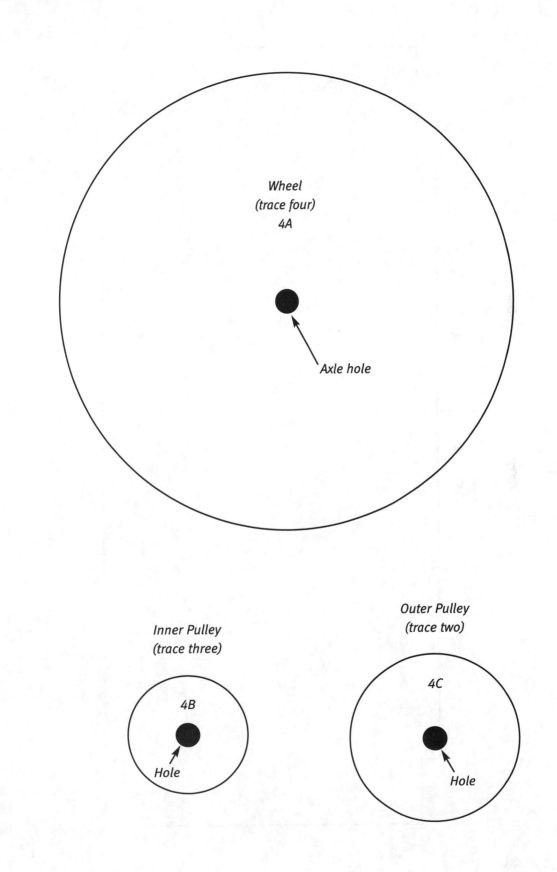

Wheel
(trace four)
4A

Axle hole

Inner Pulley
(trace three)

4B

Hole

Outer Pulley
(trace two)

4C

Hole

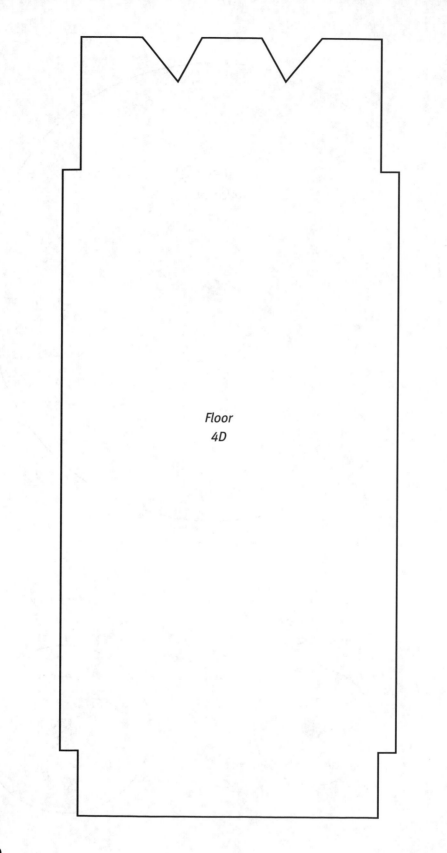

Floor
4D

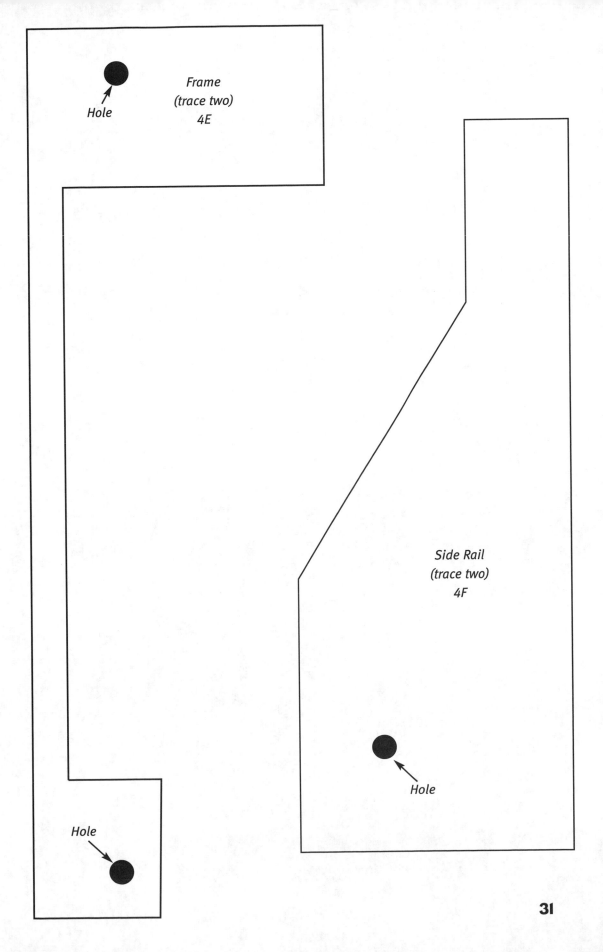

Frame
(trace two)
4E

Hole

Hole

Side Rail
(trace two)
4F

Hole

Hole

31

Simple Two-Wheeled Car

In this chapter you will build a simple two-wheeled car.

Materials and Tools

1/8-inch-thick
    corrugated
    cardboard
Scissors
3 round pencils
White glue
3 rubber bands
2 3-ounce fish-
    ing weights
Paper clip

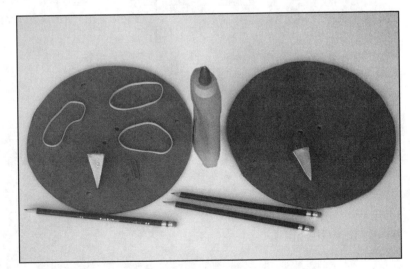

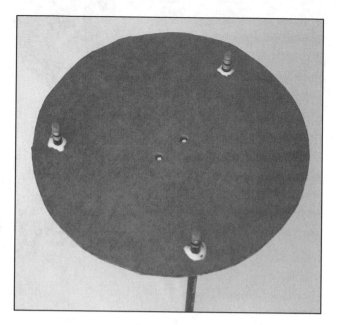

Copy the template on page 37 onto cardboard. You will need to cut out two **Wheels** (5A). Use a pencil to punch five holes in each wheel where shown.

Insert a pencil into each of the three holes near the edge of a wheel and glue them into place.

Insert the other end of the three pencils into the other wheel. Be sure the center holes in the wheels are parallel, then glue the pencils into place.

Loop three rubber bands together in a chain.

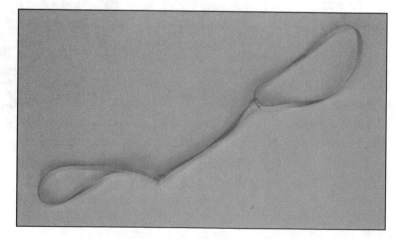

Insert the rubber band chain through one of the two center holes in the right wheel.

Pull the rubber band chain through the loop in one of the fishing weights, then through the matching hole in the left wheel.

Pull the rubber band chain back through the other hole in the left wheel. Slide the end of the last rubber band through one end of the paper clip, as shown below. Then bring the other end of the rubber band chain through the remaining hole in the right wheel. Thread this rubber band end through the weight and connect it to the other end of the paper clip.

To wind the car, slowly roll the wheels in either direction. The force of gravity will prevent the weights from turning, and this causes the rubber band to wind up. When you release the wheels, the car will roll to return to its original position.

Decorating the Car

Materials and Tools

Small circular mirrors
Colored card stock
Acrylic paints
Paintbrushes
Water
White glue
Scissors

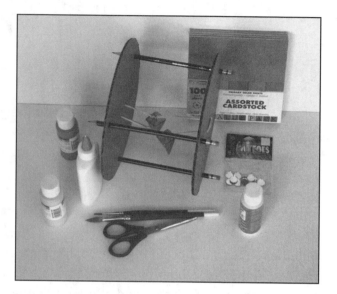

Use mirrors, colored paper, paint, or whatever else you can find to decorate your Simple Two-Wheeled Car. Here is one possible design on a finished car.

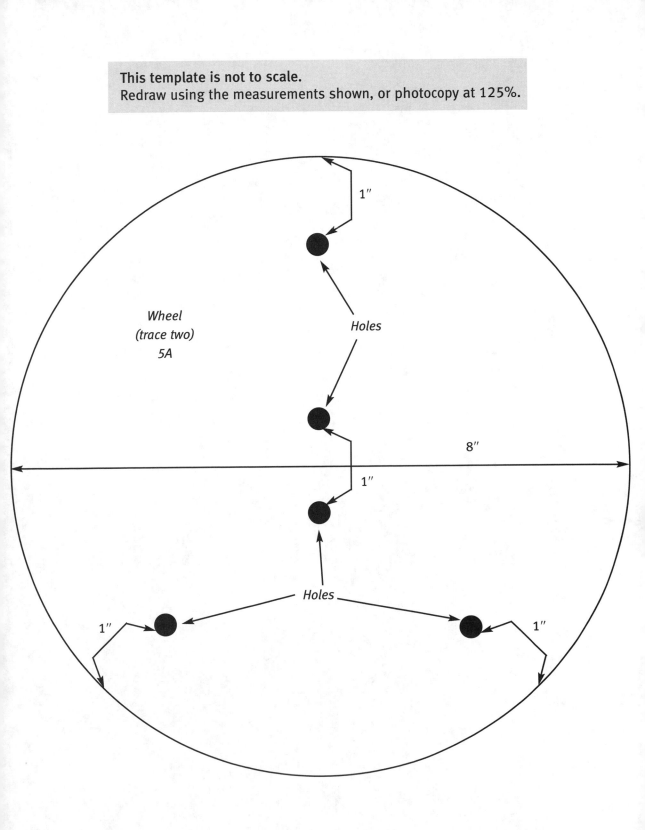

Wheel
(trace two)
5A

1″

Holes

8″

1″

Holes

1″

1″

Railroad Push Car

Materials and Tools

1/8-inch-thick corrugated
    cardboard
Scissors
White glue
Hole punch

3 round pencils
Pushpin
2 large paper clips
2 rubber bands

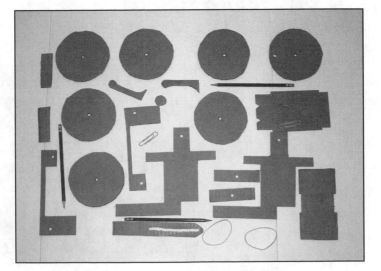

Copy the templates from pages 47, 48, 49 and 50 onto cardboard. You will need one **Top Floor** (6A), two **End Caps** (6B), two **Push Rods** (6C), two **Little People** (6D), one **Lifter Bar** (6E), one **Special Wheel** (6F), one **Washer** (6H), five **Wheels** (6G), and two **Side Rails** (6I).

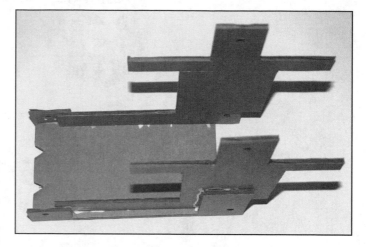

You will also need to cut one **Floor** (1A) and two **Frames** (1B) from the templates found in chapter 1, on page 11.

Glue the two frame pieces to the floor as you did in chapter 1, then glue the new side rails (6I) to the frame pieces, as shown.

Add the top floor to connect the tops of the two side rails.

Glue the two end caps to the front and rear of the top floor.

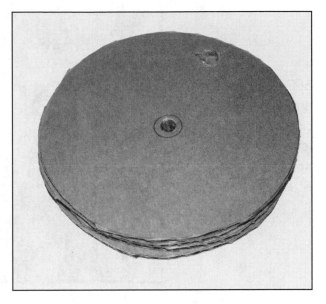

Glue two wheels and the special wheel together, with the special wheel on the outside. Be sure their center holes align.

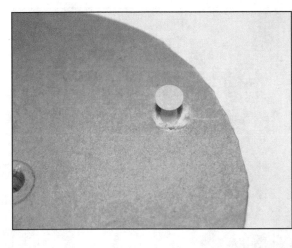

Place glue in the outer hole of the special wheel. Insert a pushpin into the hole with the glue. The top of the pushpin should stick out from the special wheel, as shown in the photo.

Insert a pencil axle through the entire wheel assembly and coat the eraser end with glue.

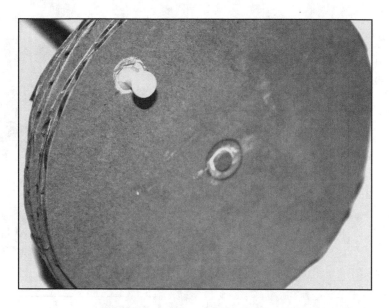

Before the glue dries, push the pencil in until the eraser is flush with (does not stick out of) the wheel.

Insert the pencil axle through the holes at the back of the frame, and glue a wheel to the other end of the axle.

Place two wheels onto a pencil axle in the front part of the frame.

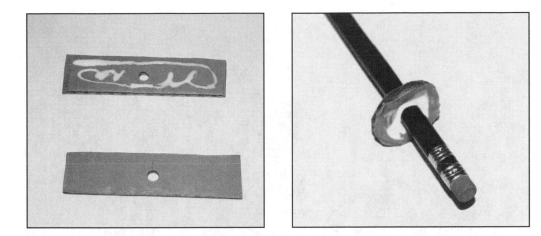

Glue the two push rod pieces together, as shown, and glue the washer onto the remaining pencil, near the eraser.

Starting on the side of the car opposite the special wheel, push the pencil (with the washer) through the hole in the upper part of the side rail, through the push rod, and through the hole on the opposite side rail. When you have centered the push rod between the side rails, as shown here, glue it in place.

Slide the lifter bar slot over the pushpin on the special wheel. Then push the hole on the lifter bar over the end of the pencil.

Be sure that the pushpin is at the bottom point of the special wheel and that the push rod, on top, is level. Now glue the upper hole in the lifter bar to the pencil. Let it dry.

Glue the two little people to the upper floor, each facing the push rod from either end. Bend the paper clips loosely around the push rod and attach them to the little people, as shown in the photo. The paper clips are the little people's arms.

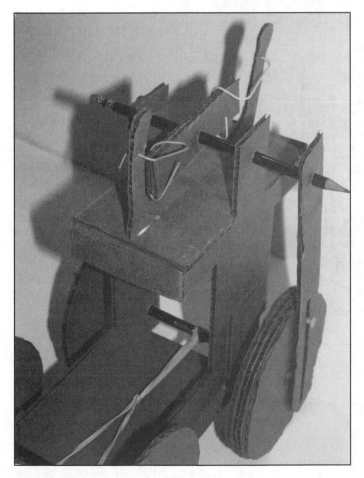

Attach rubber bands to the axle, just as you have on earlier cars, and your railroad push car is ready.

Decorating the Car

Materials and Tools

Acrylic paints
Paintbrushes
Water
Markers

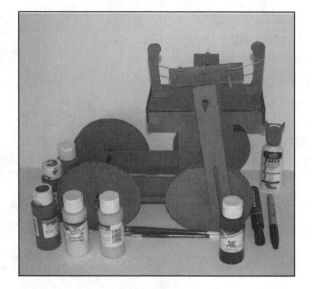

Use paint, markers, and your imagination to decorate your railroad push car. Here is one possible design.

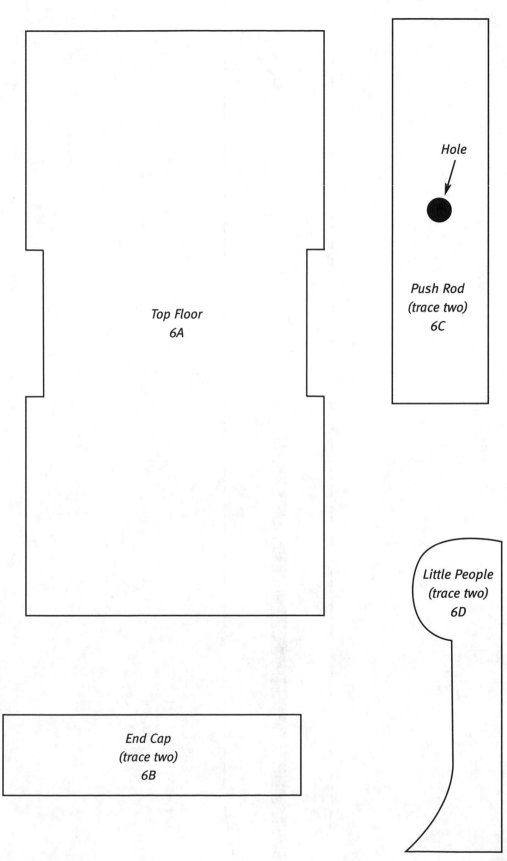

Top Floor
6A

Push Rod
(trace two)
6C

Hole

Little People
(trace two)
6D

End Cap
(trace two)
6B

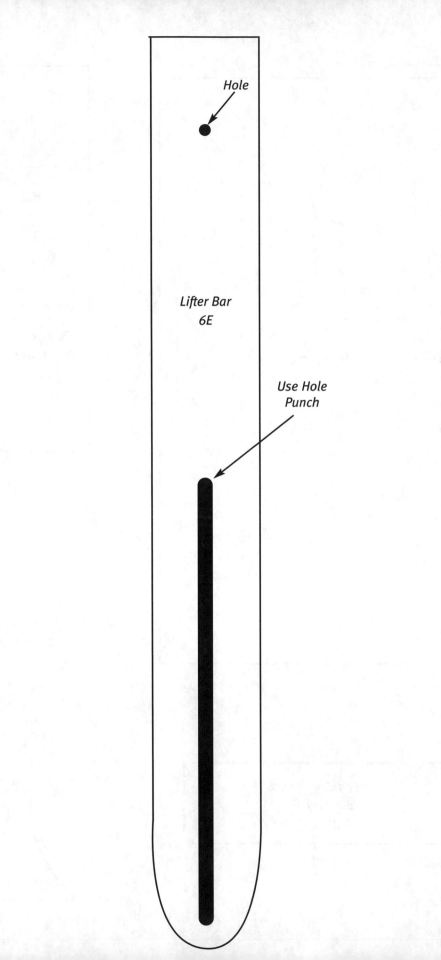

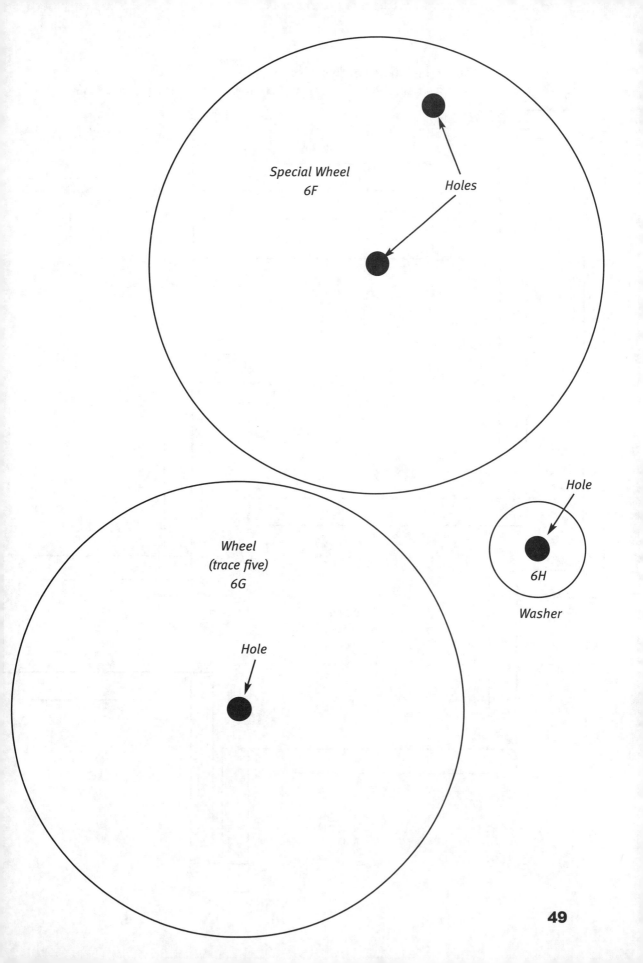

Special Wheel
6F

Holes

Hole

6H

Washer

Wheel
(trace five)
6G

Hole

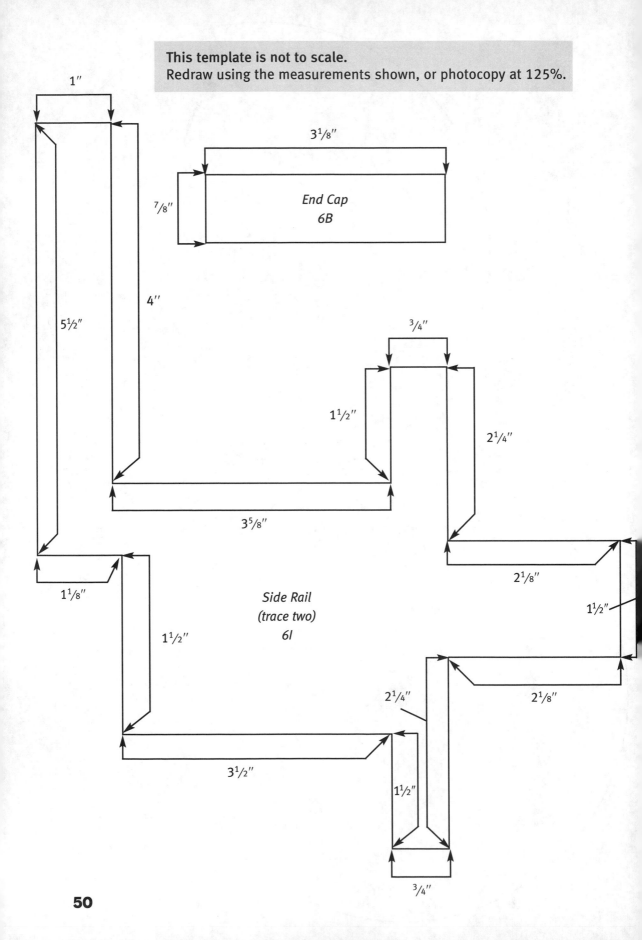

This template is not to scale.
Redraw using the measurements shown, or photocopy at 125%.

1″

3⅛″

End Cap
6B

⅞″

4″

5½″

¾″

1½″

2¼″

3⅝″

Side Rail
(trace two)
6I

2⅛″

1⅛″

1½″

1½″

2¼″

2⅛″

3½″

1½″

¾″

Oscar the Moving Clown's Body

In this chapter you build a two-wheeled car that will serves as the body for a "robot" clown—Oscar.

Materials and Tools

$\frac{1}{8}$-inch-thick corrugated
    cardboard
Scissors
Round pencil
White glue
4 C-cell batteries
2 rubber bands

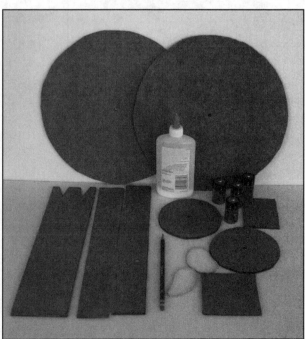

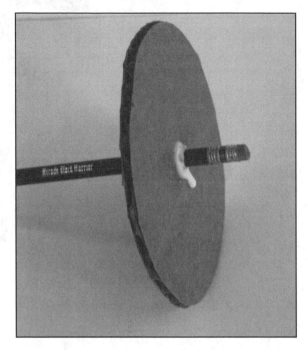

Copy the templates from pages 55 and 56 onto cardboard. You will need two **Large Wheels** (7A), two **Small Wheels** (7B), one **Bottom** (7C), one **Front** (7D), one **Back** (7E), and two **Side Rails** (7F). Now take one small wheel and attach it, using glue, to a pencil as shown.

Add glue to the inside surface of the small wheel, then glue a large wheel to the small wheel.

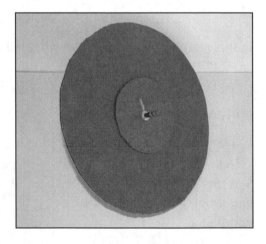

Next, glue together the back, two side rails, and bottom as shown. Be sure the back's notches are at the open end, and that the two holes on the side rails are closer to the base (away from the notches). Also, the side rails must rest *on top of* the back, while the bottom is glued at the end of the back and side rails. Look carefully at the photo before you start gluing.

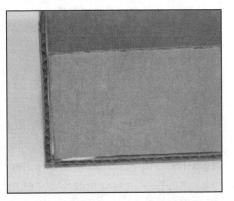

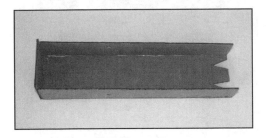

Glue the front onto the tops of the side rails. The front is located on the end away from the notches.

Slide the pencil-and-wheel assembly through the holes in the side rails.

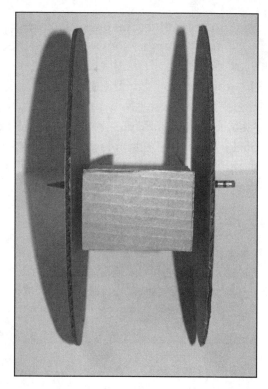

Make another double wheel by gluing the remaining large and small wheels together. Slide it over the other end of the pencil, with the small wheel to the outside, and glue it into place. Note that the center piece will lay on the table instead of standing straight up.

When all the glue is dry, place the C-cell batteries into the bottom of the center piece.

Finally, attach one end of the rubber band chain to the pencil axle and the other end through the notches on the back piece.

A photo of the complete, decorated clown is shown at the end of chapter 9.

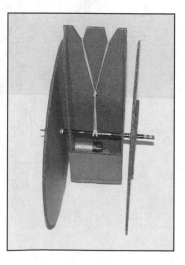

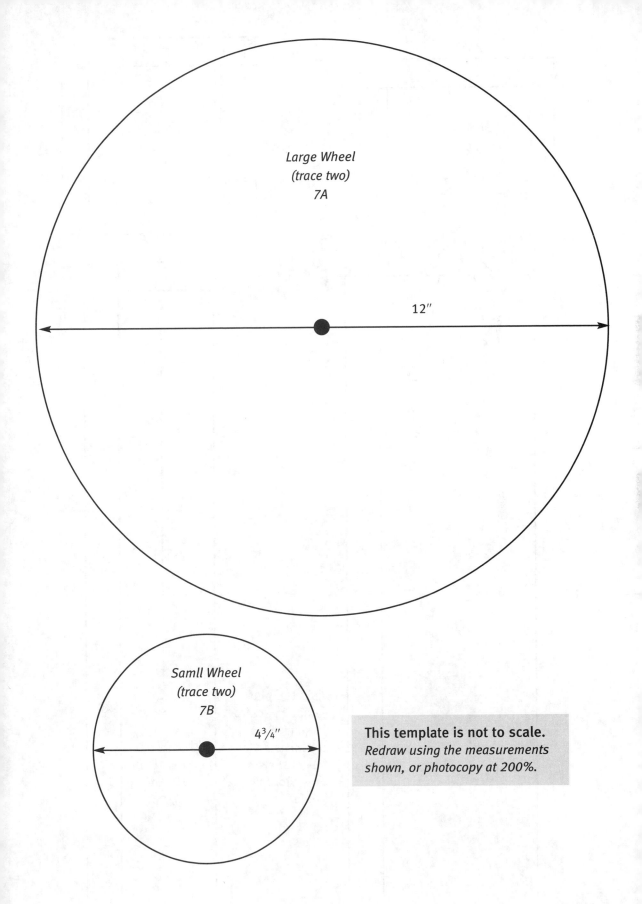

Large Wheel
(trace two)
7A

12″

Samll Wheel
(trace two)
7B

4³/₄″

This template is not to scale.
Redraw using the measurements shown, or photocopy at 200%.

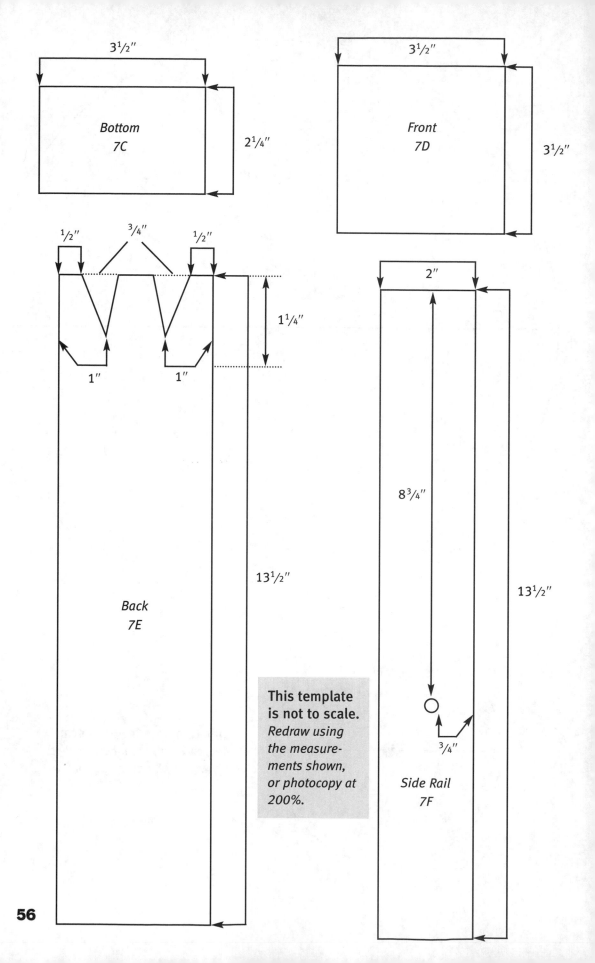

3½"

Bottom
7C

2¼"

3½"

Front
7D

3½"

½"　　　¾"　　½"

1¼"

1"　　　1"

13½"

Back
7E

2"

8¾"

¾"

Side Rail
7F

13½"

This template is not to scale. *Redraw using the measurements shown, or photocopy at 200%.*

8

Oscar the Moving Clown's Head

In this chapter you will build a movable head to add to the two-wheeled vehicle body from the previous chapter. When you are finished, the mouth on this head will open and close and the eyes will blink when Oscar is in motion.

Materials and Tools

⅛-inch-thick corrugated
    cardboard
Paper
Scissors
White glue
2 pushpins
Round pencil
Black marker
4 D-cell batteries (to hold
    the pieces in place
    while the glue dries)
Oscar's body (from
    chapter 7)

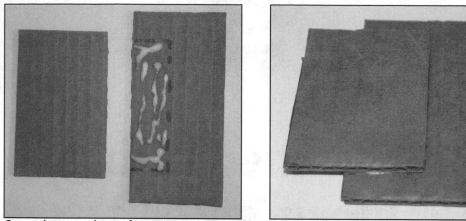

Copy the templates from pages 66 and 67 onto cardboard, except for the eyes. You will need one **Jaw Brace** (8A), one **Jaw Support** (8B), one **Base** (8C), one **Jaw Lifter** (8D), two **Lower Jaws** (8E), two **Jaw Stops** (8F), two **Top of Heads** (8H), and two **Upper Jaws** (8I). Trace the two **Eyes** (8G) onto paper.

Glue the jaw support onto the base, taking care to position the support on the dotted lines on the base, as shown.

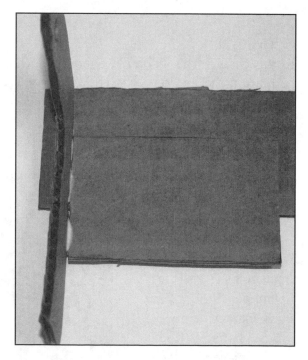

Using a pushpin and pencil, make holes in the upper jaw and lower jaw. Now glue one of the lower jaws to the jaw support and base.

Glue the other lower jaw to the jaw support and base on the opposite side.

Glue the jaw brace between the back of the lower jaws, as shown in the photo. This will complete Oscar's lower jaw. Let the glue dry.

Take the paper eye and color it with a black marker.

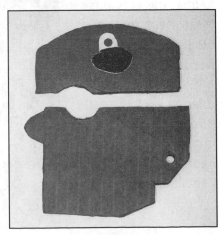

Attach the eye to the back side of the top of the head piece using a pushpin. Do not push the pushpin in so far that the eye does not swing freely.

Glue the top of the head to the upper jaw. Use the D-cell batteries to hold the top of the head and upper jaw together while the glue dries.

Repeat the previous three steps for the other side of the head.

After the glue dries, insert a pencil through one of the upper jaws and glue it near the end of the pencil, as shown.

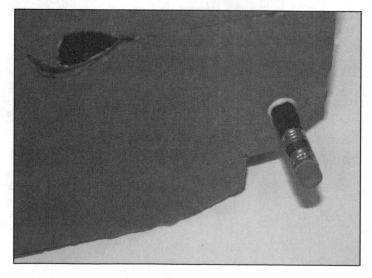

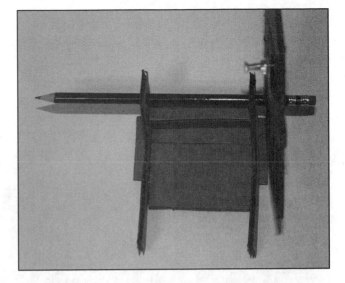

Slide the pencil from the upper jaw and head through the holes on the lower jaw you built earlier.

Push the other upper jaw and head onto the pencil and glue it in place. The pushpins should be facing one another, on the inside of Oscar's head.

Now it's time to install the jaw stop. The jaw stop determines the closed position of Oscar's mouth. Glue a jaw stop onto the lower jaw on both sides of Oscar's head.

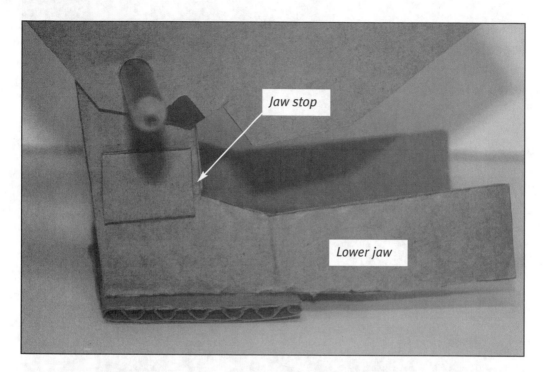

Jaw stop

Lower jaw

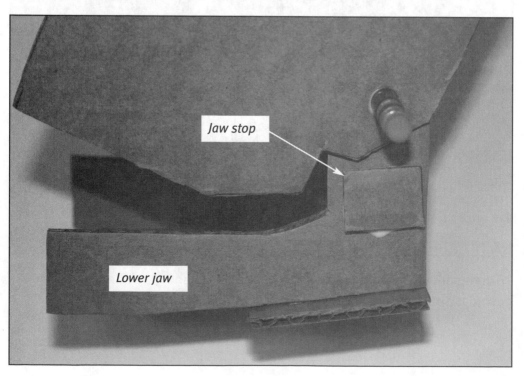

Jaw stop

Lower jaw

The upper jaw should rest on the jaw stops when Oscar's mouth is closed.

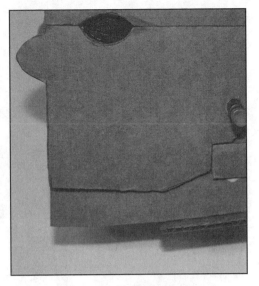

Now you will attach Oscar's head to the top of the body you made in the previous chapter. (Note: it is easier to decorate the body, particularly the neck, *before* attaching the head to it.)

Place glue on the top two edges of the side rails on the body.

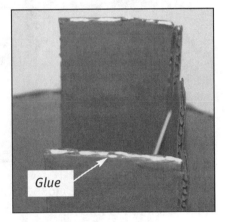

Glue

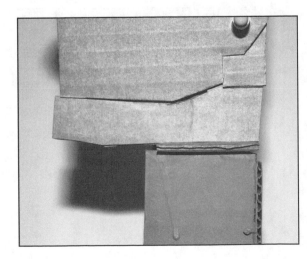

Attach Oscar's head to the top of the body. Do not use glue on the back of the body, where the notches are, just in case you need to replace the rubber band in the future. Hold the head assembly to the body while the glue dries.

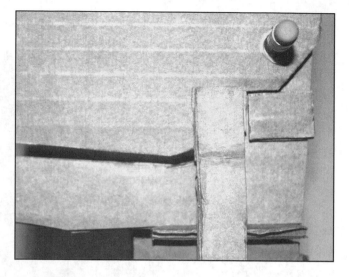

Glue the jaw lifter onto the *upper* jaw, as shown.

Insert a pushpin into the wheel near the lower end of the jaw lifter. The pushpin will cause the jaw lifter to rise when the wheel turns forward.

Oscar's eyes should be closed when his head is down, but be partially open when his head is raised.

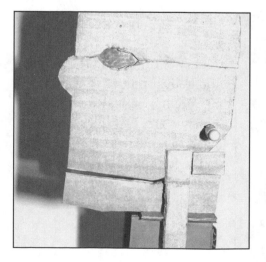

To make Oscar move, tilt his head backward (important, or the pushpin will bend the jaw lifter!) and wind the wheels backward. Then gently lower Oscar's head and release the wheels to see this clown in action!

Decorating Oscar

Materials and Tools

Acrylic paint
Paintbrushes
Water
Black marker
White glue
Fiberfill or cotton balls

You can decorate Oscar however you'd like. Here's one idea for a finished head.

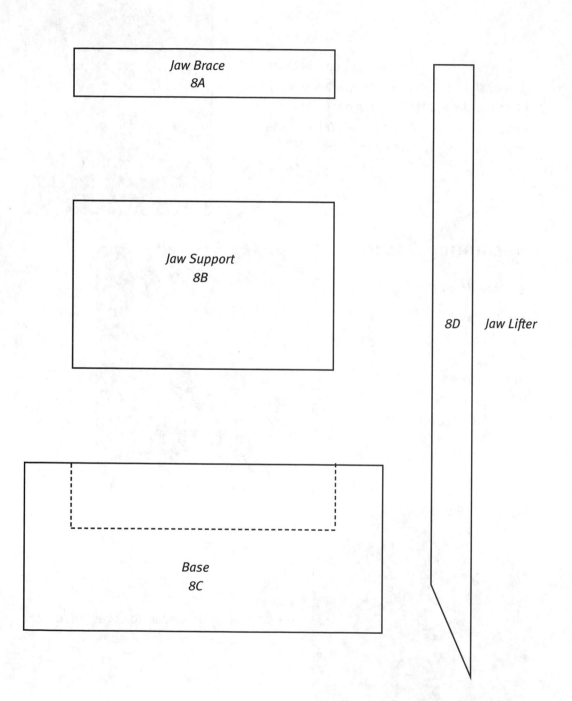

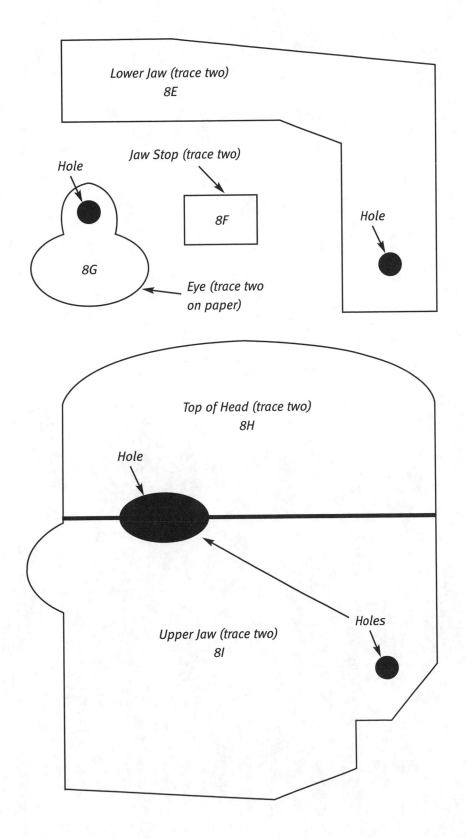

Steering for Oscar

In this chapter you will add a steering wheel to Oscar the clown.

Materials and Tools

¹⁄₈-inch-thick corrugated
    cardboard
Scissors
White glue
Paper clip
Round pencil
Oscar's head and body
    from chapter 8

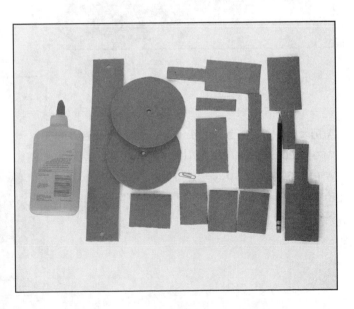

Copy the templates from
pages 75 and 76 onto
cardboard. You will need
one **Wheel Support
Spacer** (9A), one **Base**
(9B), three **Upright Supports** (9C), one **Brace** (9D), four **Wheel Supports** (9E),
and one **Axle Support** (9F). You will also need to cut two **Wheels** (1D) from the
template found in chapter 1, on page 12.

First, place glue on one of the wheel support pieces.

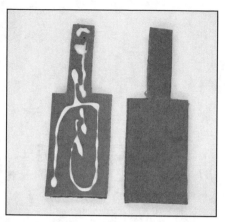

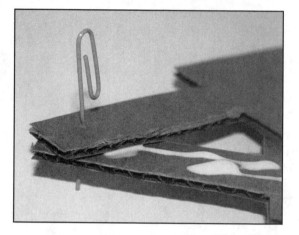

Insert one end of a paper clip through the hole at the end of two wheel support pieces (one with glue and one without) before sliding them together.

Add glue to the bottom, wide part of these two pieces, as shown. Then place the wheel support spacer on top of the two glued wheel supports from the previous step.

Finally, glue a third and fourth wheel support to the other side of the spacer, keeping the paper clip in the hole. Look carefully at the photo before you start gluing. This is the completed wheel support assembly.

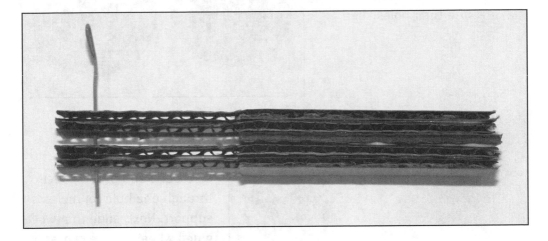

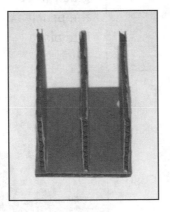

Glue the three upright supports to the base, as shown.

Glue the base assembly to the wheel support assembly.

Glue the two wheels together, making sure their holes align.

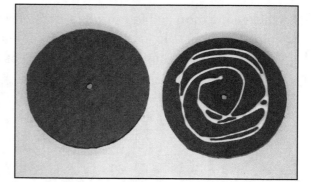

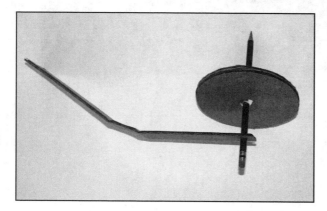

Insert one end of the pencil through one hole on the axle support. Next, slide the two glued wheels to the center of the pencil axle and glue them into place.

Bend the axle support at the "bend lines" and push the other end of the pencil through the second hole in the axle support.

Once the axle support is in place, glue the brace across the axle support.

Now take the wheel support and base assembly and glue it to Oscar's body, six inches from the lower end of the body.

Pull out the paper clip from the wheel support assembly, slide the axle support into the slot, and reinsert the paper clip, as shown.

Oscar's now complete! If you turn the rear steering wheel, it will cause Oscar to move in a circle. If you align the steering wheel with the large wheel, he will move forward in a straight line.

When you are sure Oscar is working the way you'd like, finish decorating him. Here's how I did it.

Wheel Support Spacer
9A

Upright Support
(trace three)
9C

Base
9B

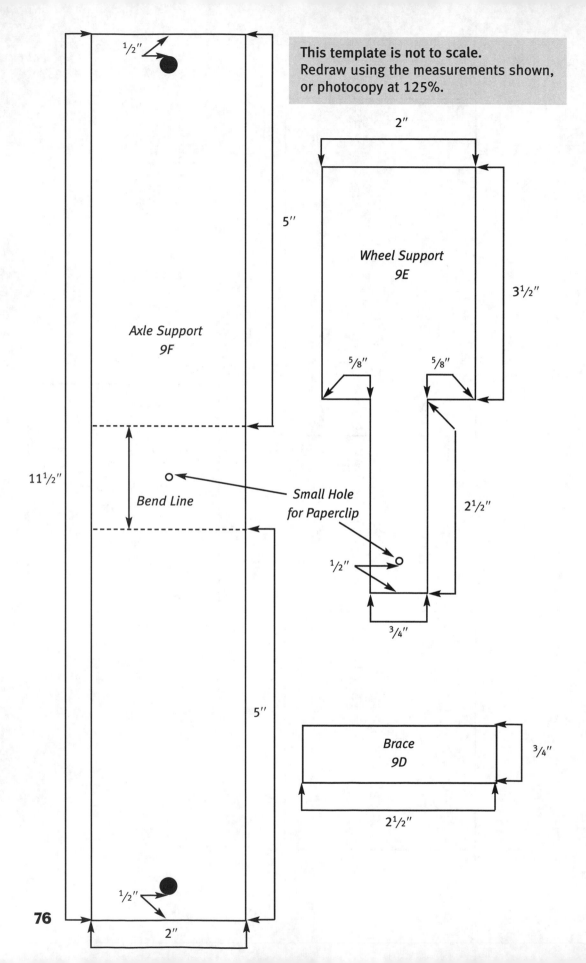

This template is not to scale.
Redraw using the measurements shown,
or photocopy at 125%.

1/2"

2"

5"

Wheel Support
9E

3 1/2"

Axle Support
9F

5/8"   5/8"

11 1/2"

Bend Line

Small Hole
for Paperclip

2 1/2"

1/2"

3/4"

5"

Brace
9D

3/4"

2 1/2"

1/2"

76

2"

Domino Cars

In this chapter you will build a car that will sit in place, even though its rubber band is wound up, waiting for the arrival of another car. When the first car hits the second, it will take off—domino cars!

Materials and Tools

Basic Rubber Band Car
    (from Chapter 1)
⅛-inch-thick corrugated cardboard
Scissors
Pushpin

White glue
2 round pencils
2 rubber bands
D-cell battery

Set aside the already made Basic Rubber Band Car. Use the templates and directions found in chapter 1 to make a second Basic Rubber Band Car, but use the **Special Wheel** template (10A) on page 81 for this car's right rear wheel. This special wheel is notched.

Now it's time to build the Domino Car Launcher. Copy the templates from pages 81, 82, and 83 onto cardboard. You will need one **Bumper** (10B), one **Transfer Beam** (10C), and one **Wheel Block** (10D).

Bend the transfer beam *up* along Bend Line A and *down* along Bend Line B. Then glue the Bend Line A section to the bumper piece, as shown.

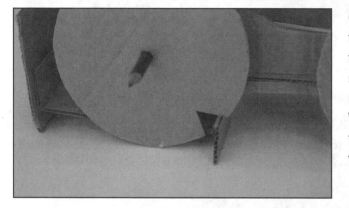

Glue the wheel block to the front right corner of the Bend Line B section, so that it sticks out to the right, as in the photo here. When the car is wound, the wheel block will prevent the car from moving.

Place a D-cell battery in the back of the car, near the right wheel, to prevent it from jumping over the wheel block.

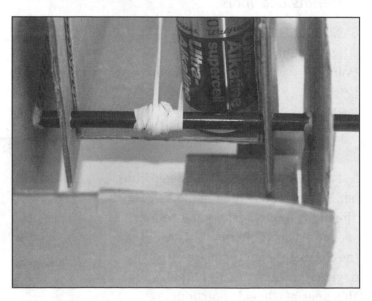

Wind up the rubber band on the rear axle and place the car on the Domino Car Launcher. With the bumper and wheel block in place, the car is ready to go. Now, when a second car strikes the bumper from behind, the car with the special wheel will take off.

Decorating the Car

Materials and Tools

Acrylic paint
Paintbrushes
Water
Markers

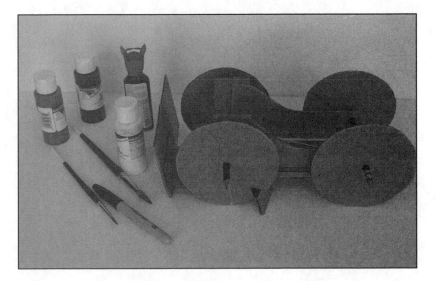

Use paint and markers to decorate the Domino Car. I painted a target on the Domino Car Launcher's bumper, and a domino theme on the car itself.

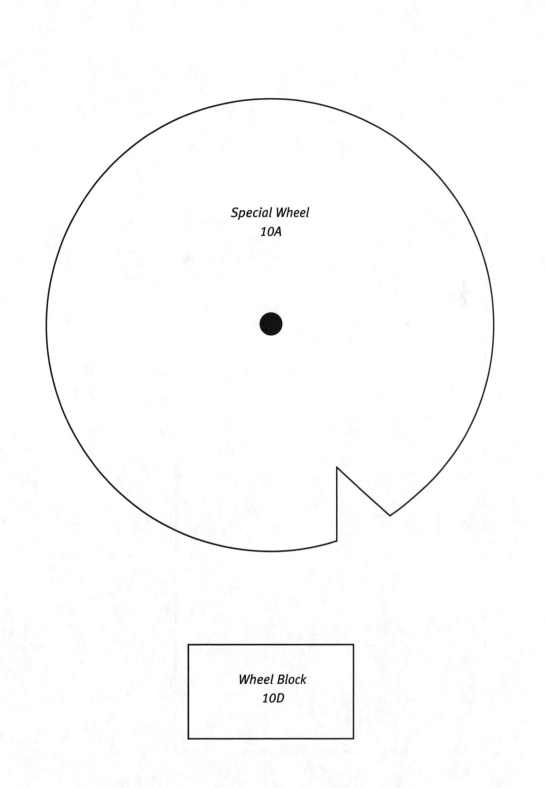

Special Wheel
10A

Wheel Block
10D

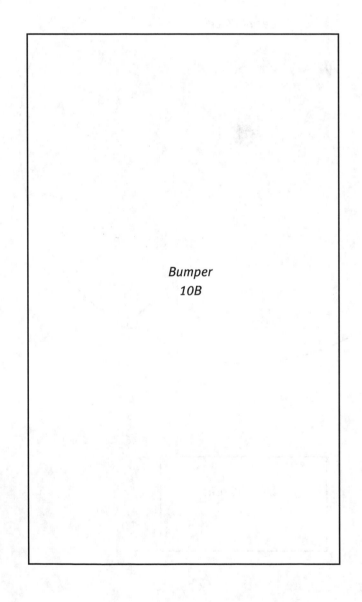

Bumper
10B

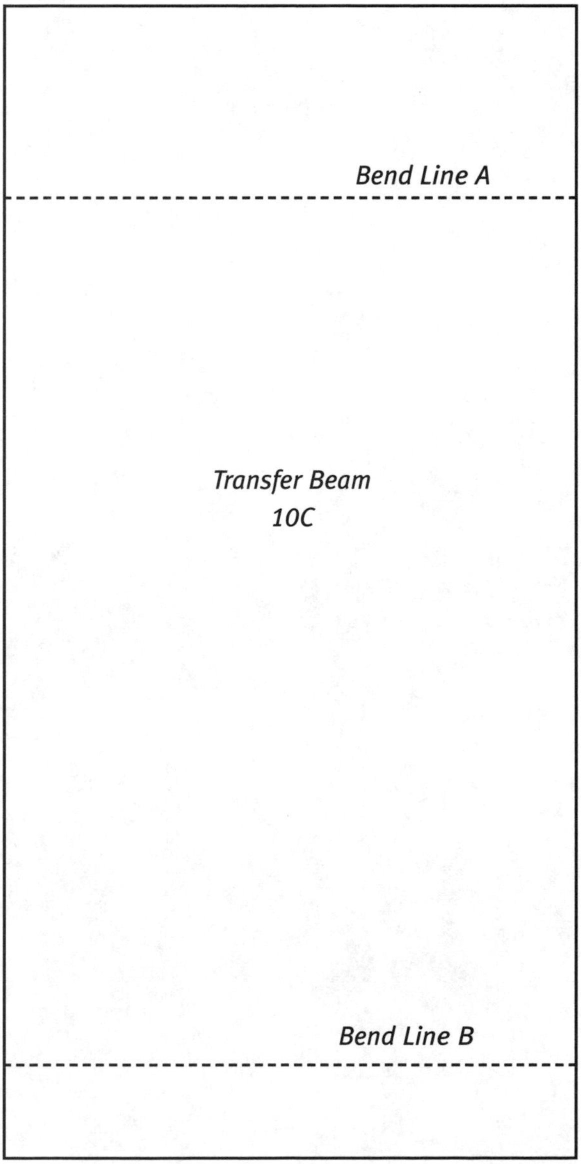

Bend Line A

Transfer Beam
10C

Bend Line B

High-Speed Car

In this chapter you will make a fast car. Two sets of rubber bands will provide the power for its large rear wheels.

Materials and Tools

1/8-inch-thick cor-
     rugated card-
     board
Scissors
White glue
2 round pencils
4 rubber bands

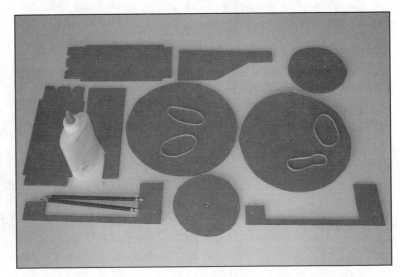

Copy the templates from pages 89, 90, and 91 onto cardboard. You will need two **Large Rear Wheels** (11A), two **Front Wheels** (11B), two **Floors** (11C), two **Frames** (11D), and two **Side Rails** (11E).

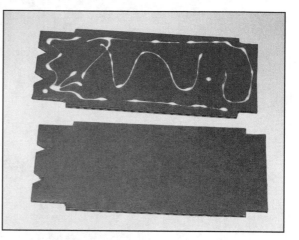

Start by gluing the two floor pieces together. This will make a strong base for the rubber bands to pull against.

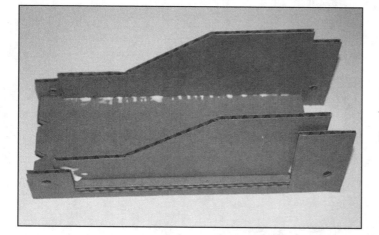

Use glue to add the frame and side rail pieces to the floor.

Mount the two large rear wheels on a pencil axle and glue them in place.

Glue the front wheels to the second pencil axle.

Take one rubber band chain and loop it around the rear axle. Fasten the other end of this chain to the front of the car. Take the second rubber band chain and loop it around the rear axle (next to the first chain). Fasten the other end of this chain to the front of the car, on top of the first chain.

Decorating the Car

Materials and Tools

Felt star stickers
Stripe stickers
Scissors
Acrylic paint
Paintbrushes
Water

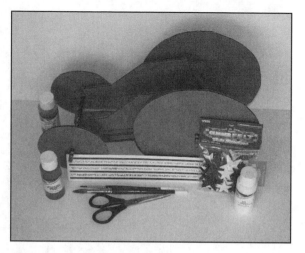

Use felt stickers, paint, and stripe stickers to decorate your High-Speed Car. Here is one example of a completed car.

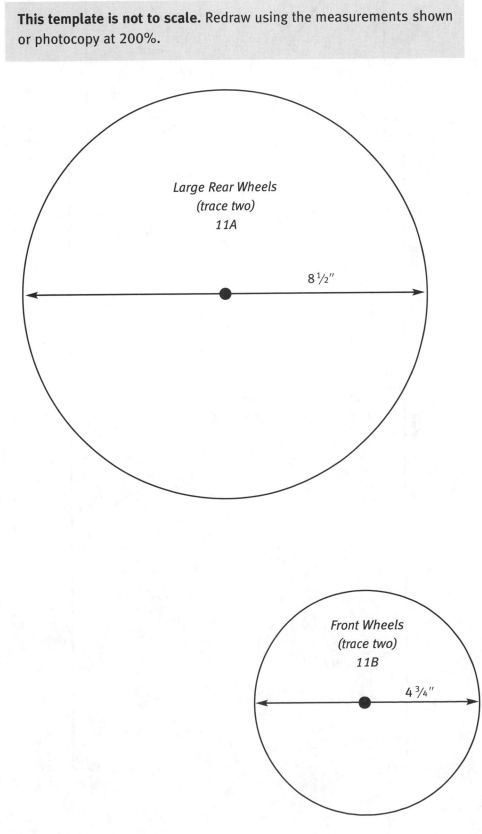

Large Rear Wheels
(trace two)
11A

8 ½″

Front Wheels
(trace two)
11B

4 ¾″

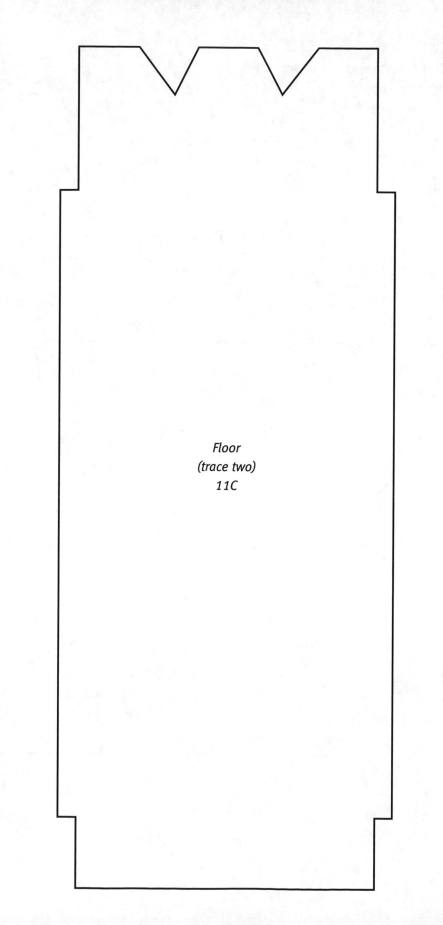

Floor
(trace two)
11C

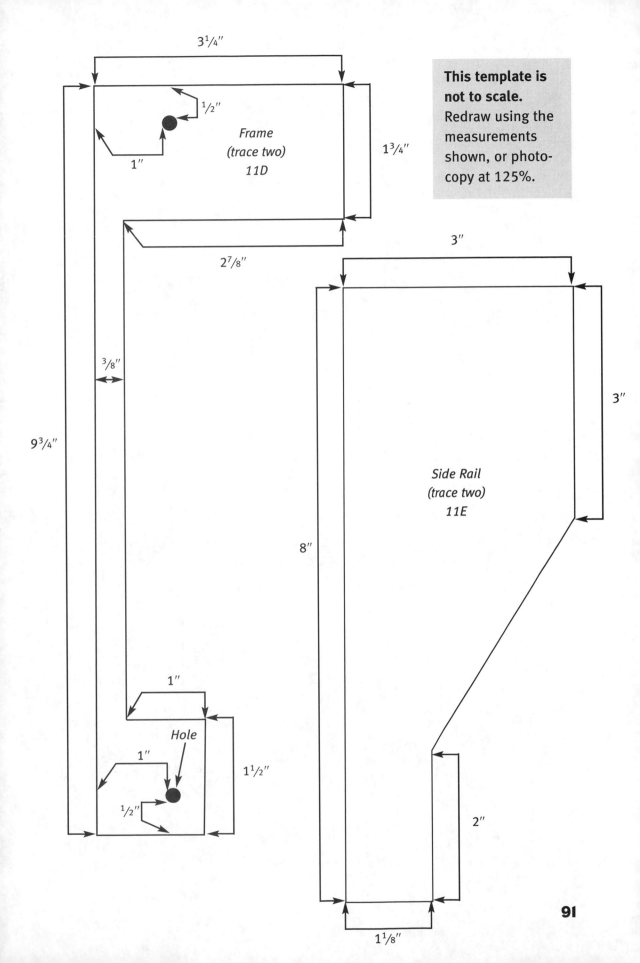

3¼"

This template is not to scale. Redraw using the measurements shown, or photocopy at 125%.

½"

Frame
(trace two)
11D

1¾"

1"

2⁷⁄₈"

3"

⅜"

9¾"

3"

Side Rail
(trace two)
11E

8"

1"

Hole

1"

1½"

½"

2"

1⅛"

Spot, the Dog with the Wagging Tail

In this chapter you will build Spot, a cardboard dog with floppy ears. Spot is powered by rubber bands and will wag his tail up and down after being pulled back and released.

Materials and Tools

⅛-inch-thick corrugated
    cardboard
Scissors
2 pushpins
Hole punch
White glue
2 round pencils
Pipe cleaner
2 rubber bands

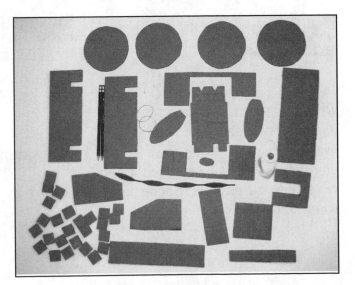

Copy the templates from pages 106 through 110 onto cardboard. You will need two **Frames** (12A), one **Floor** (12B), two **Side Rails** (12C), one **Head—Lower Piece** (12D), four **Wheels** (12E), one **Body—Rear** (12F), one **Tail Support** (12G), one **Tail Lifter** (12H), one **Body Top** (12I), twenty-six **Squares** (12J), one **Head—Upper Piece** (12K), one **Body—Front** (12L), two **Ears** (12M), and two **Head—Sides** (12N).

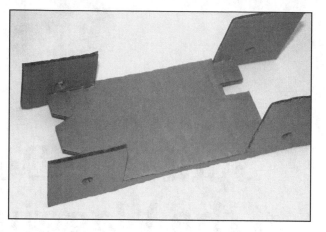

Make holes in the wheels and frames as shown in chapter 1, pages 2 and 3. Use a hole punch to make a hole in the tail lifter.

After all holes have been made, glue the two frame pieces to the floor.

Next, glue the side rails to the inside of the frames.

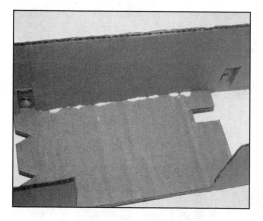 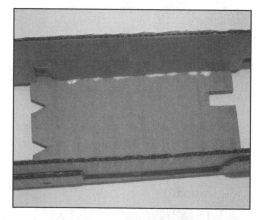

While the glue dries on the side rails and frames, push one of the wheels over a pencil and slide it close to the eraser end. Place glue around the pencil close to the eraser and slide the wheel into place over the glue.

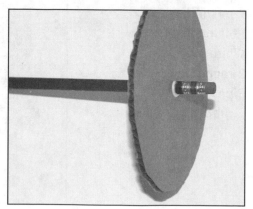

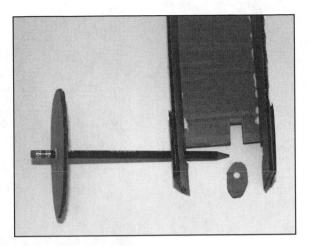

Insert the pencil axle through one hole at the back end of the frame.

Slide the tail lifter onto the pencil before the pencil axle is pushed through the second hole in the frame.

With the wheel in the location shown, place glue on the pencil to line up with the slot in the floor.

Move the tail lifter onto the glue, then add a second wheel to the pencil axle and glue it $\frac{1}{2}$ inch away from the frame.

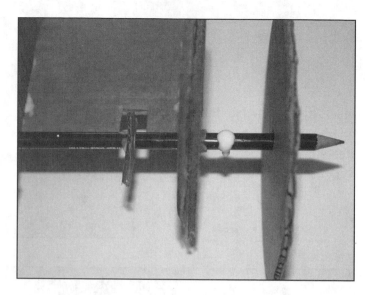

Slide the wheel onto the glue.

Add two wheels and an axle to the front of the frame.

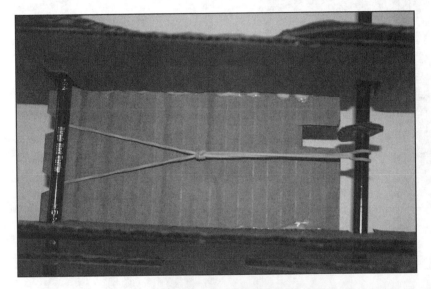

Attach the rubber bands to the pencil and floor. (Follow the instructions on pages 5 through 8.)

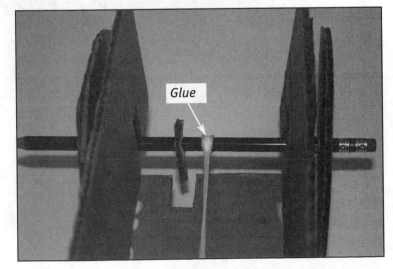

Glue

Now add a drop of glue to the rubber band at the pencil and let it dry.

Glue the pipe-cleaner tail to the end of the tail support. Bend the tail so that it will come out of the center of the dog. Glue the tail support (with the tail) to the floor. The middle of the tail support must rest on top of the tail lifter so that the tail will rise and fall as the dog moves.

Tail support goes here

Glue the body top to the side rails.

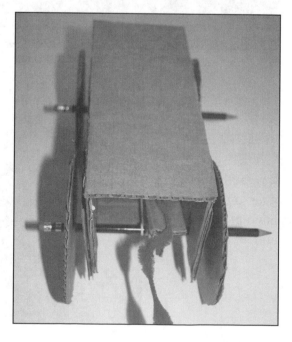

Next, glue the body—rear to the back of the car, making sure that it does not touch the tail.

Glue the body—front to the front of the car.

Now it's time to build Spot's head. Glue a lower head piece to a single head—side, as shown. Notice that one bend in the lower head piece is longer than the other.

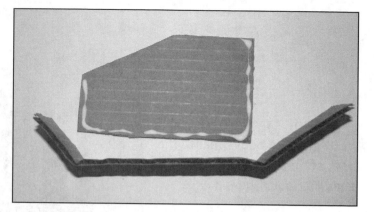

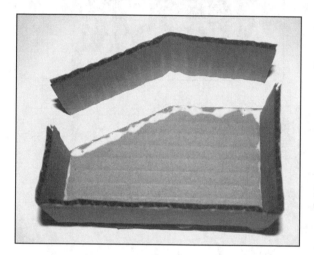

Glue the head—upper piece to the head—side and the two top edges of the lower head piece.

When the glue has dried, glue the remaining head—side to this assembly.

Now it's time to build the bases that hold the ears. You will need six squares and two pushpins. For each base, place glue on two of the squares and stick them together, then glue the third square, with a pushpin in the center, to the stack of two.

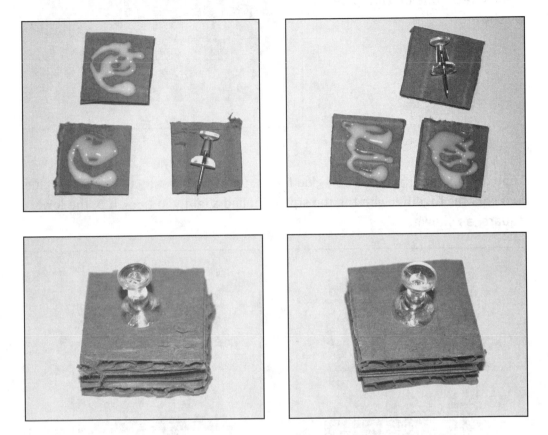

Punch a hole in the center of each of two more squares. Glue these squares to the top of the stack you made in the previous step.

Glue the bases for the ears to
Spot's head, one on each side,
as shown.

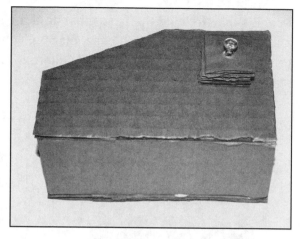

Time to build Spot's neck. First, glue four squares together in a stack. Then glue
two squares together with the top square pulled slightly to the left of the lower
square, as shown.

Continue gluing the remaining
squares together like this, and
combine them with the stack of
four squares to create the neck
shown here.

Glue the neck to the bottom of the head. (The stack of four should be at the end that is *not* glued to the head.)

Push the ears over the pushpins onto the sides of Spot's head.

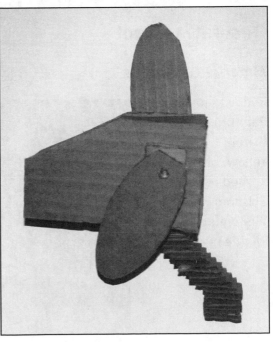

Glue the neck to the top of the body. You may have to prop it up until the glue dries completely.

Spot is now ready to run! Because the rubber band is hidden inside and glued to the pencil axle (so that the rubber band will not slip), Spot should be easy to operate. Pull him backward, then release.

Decorating Spot

Materials and Tools

Red acrylic paint
Paintbrush
Water
Yellow, black, and
    red felt
Scissors
White glue
Wiggle eyes

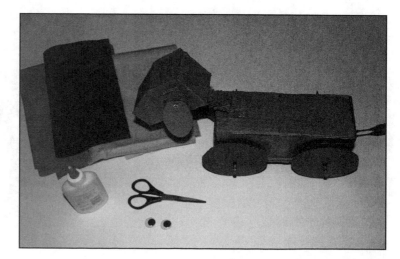

To decorate Spot, first paint his wheels red.

Cover Spot in yellow felt. For his spots and ears, cut out black and red felt pieces and glue them on. Finally, glue wiggle eyes to his head.

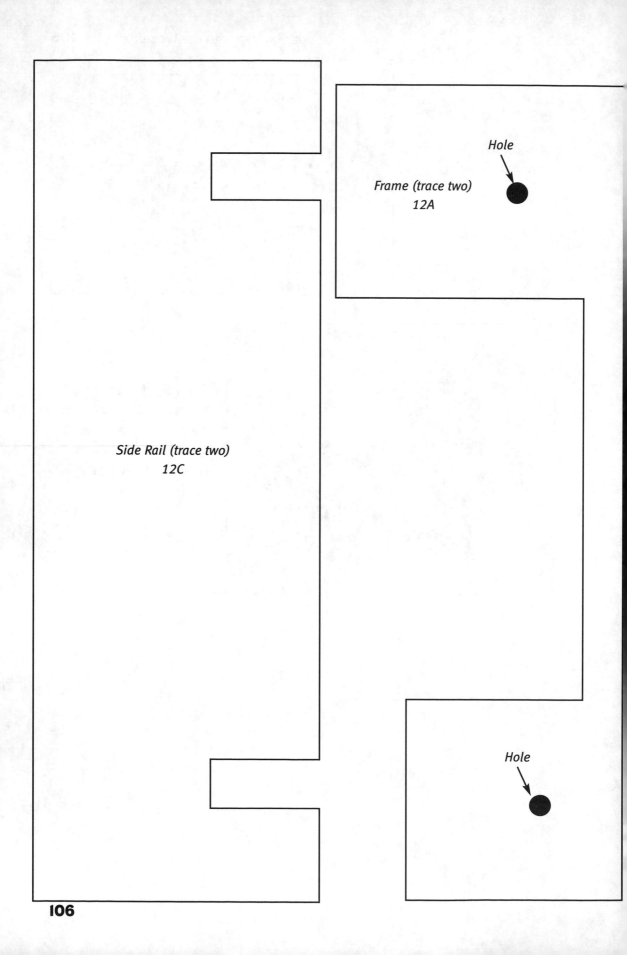

Frame (trace two)
12A

Hole

Side Rail (trace two)
12C

Hole

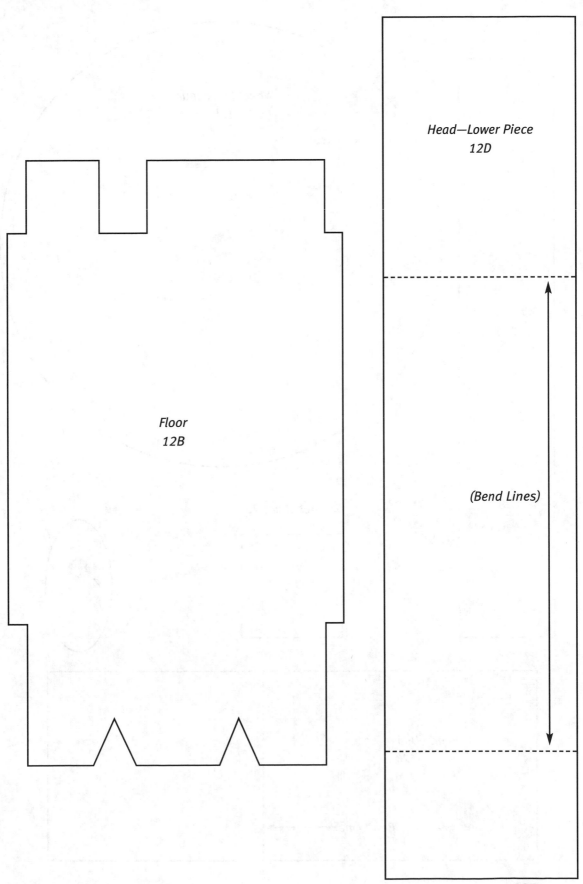

Floor
12B

Head—Lower Piece
12D

(Bend Lines)

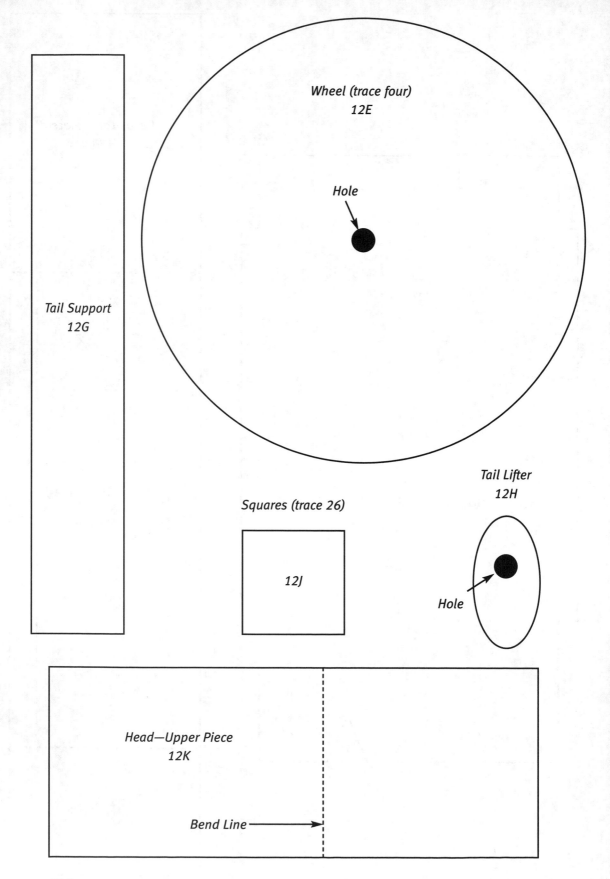

Wheel (trace four)
12E

Hole

Tail Support
12G

Tail Lifter
12H

Squares (trace 26)

12J

Hole

Head—Upper Piece
12K

Bend Line

Body Top
121

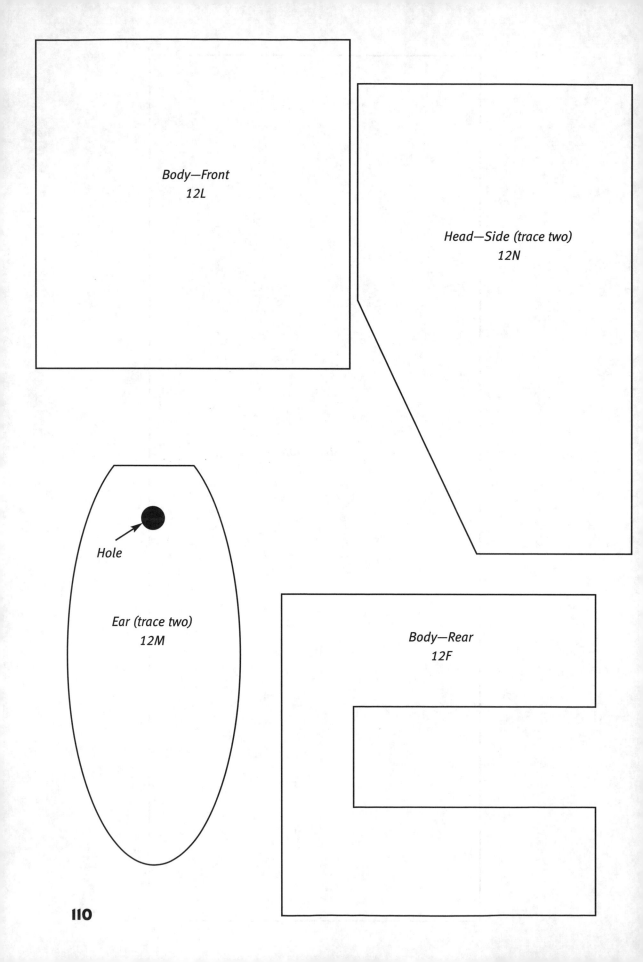

Body—Front
12L

Head—Side (trace two)
12N

Hole

Ear (trace two)
12M

Body—Rear
12F

Life-Sized Rubber Band Car

In this chapter you will build a life-sized rubber band–powered car that is capable of carrying a human. What's more, the seat on this car can be removed and used as a chair.

Materials and Tools

1/8-inch-thick corrugated cardboard
Yardstick
Compass
Scissors
White glue
Drill
2-inch drill bit
4 1-inch (inside) diameter bearings (available from VXB Ball Bearings, www.vxb.com, item "Kit 208")
3 24-inch-long, 1-inch-diameter dowels (preferable maple)
6 84-inch-long, 3/4-inch-wide rubber bands (available from Dykema Rubber Band Company, www.dykemarubberband.com, item "PalletM." Mention this book, and the 12-piece minimum on the pallet bands will be waived.

Copy the two templates from page 118 onto cardboard. You will need 16 **Bearing Holders** (13A) and 12 **Filler Rings** (13B). The remaining templates, on pages 119 through 121, are not to scale. Because the actual pieces are so large, you will not be able to simply photocopy them to the size you need. Instead, measure each template onto cardboard using a yardstick, a compass, and the measurements provided. Once the first of each template is cut out, use it to trace the remaining pieces. You will

need 10 **Frames** (13C), 78 **Floor Supports** (13D), 20 **Wheels** (13E), and 76 **Chair Pieces** (13F). As you can imagine, it may take you some time to collect enough cardboard to build this car.

Glue five frame pieces together in a stack, then add the 78 floor supports, then the final five frame pieces, to create the base shown.

Drill four 2-inch-diameter holes for the wheel bearings in the side frame, following the measurements on the template.

Slide two bearings onto a dowel and insert the dowel and bearings through the frame holes at the front (as labeled on template) of the base.

Adjust the dowel and bearings until the dowel is centered and the bearings are inside the cardboard frame holes. The bearings should be flush with the inside of the frame. The bearings will *not* be flush with the outer edge of the frame.

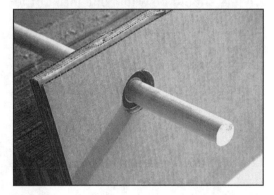

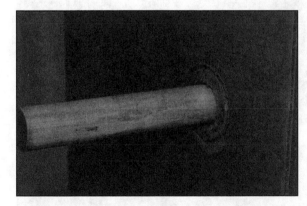

Carefully add three filler rings to the axle from each end, then slide them into the frame holes, against the bearings, until they are even with the frame. **Do NOT glue these filler rings in place.**

On the outside of the frame, glue two bearing holders around each bearing to prevent the bearing and filler rings from sliding out of the holes. On the inside of the frame, glue two bearing holders around each bearing to prevent them from sliding out of the holes. Be careful not to let any glue get on the bearings.

Build four wheels by gluing together five wheel cutouts in each stack. Once dry, glue a wheel to each end of the front axle. The wheels should be within one inch of the frame.

Attach the rubber bands to the front axle.

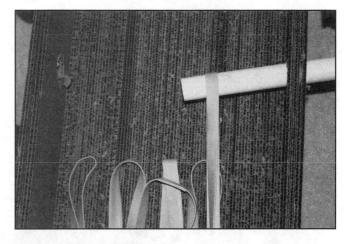

Slide another dowel through the 1-inch-diameter rubber band brace holes near the back of the car's base. While you do, thread the rubber bands over the dowel, as shown.

Now assemble the back axle and wheels using the remaining two wheels, dowel, bearings, filler rings, and bearing holders. The base of the car should look like this.

Now it's time to build the chair, which will sit on the base of the car. As you cut and glue together the 76 chair pieces, alternate the "grain" of the cardboard to add strength. To alternate the grain, make sure that the ridges in one piece of cardboard go up and down while the ridges in the next piece go left to right. After you have glued the first 70 chair pieces together, check the width of the

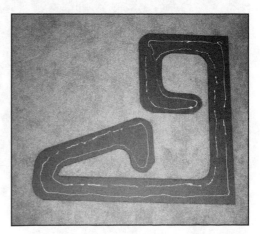

chair to be certain that it will fit into the base. Add additional chair pieces, one at a time, making certain that the chair will still fit. Do not make the chair wider than the hole it fits into.

The complete chair should look like the photo below.

Insert the chair into the base, and your car is now complete! (Do not glue it in place. You may want to remove the chair later.)

Push the car backward to wind up the rubber bands. Have a seat, and see how far you can go!

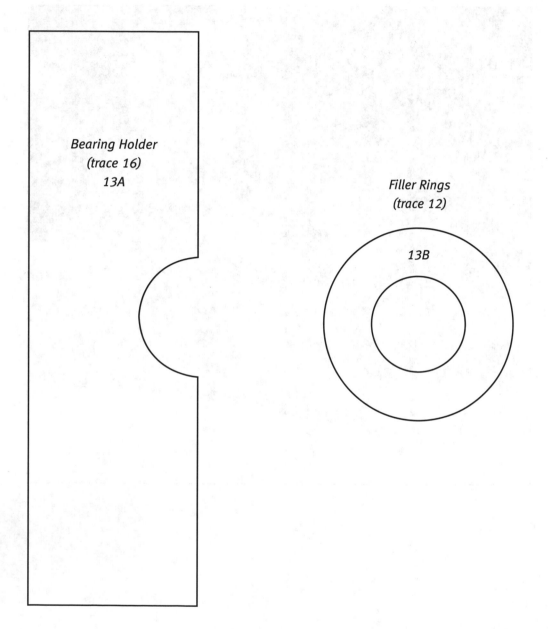

Bearing Holder
(trace 16)
13A

Filler Rings
(trace 12)

13B

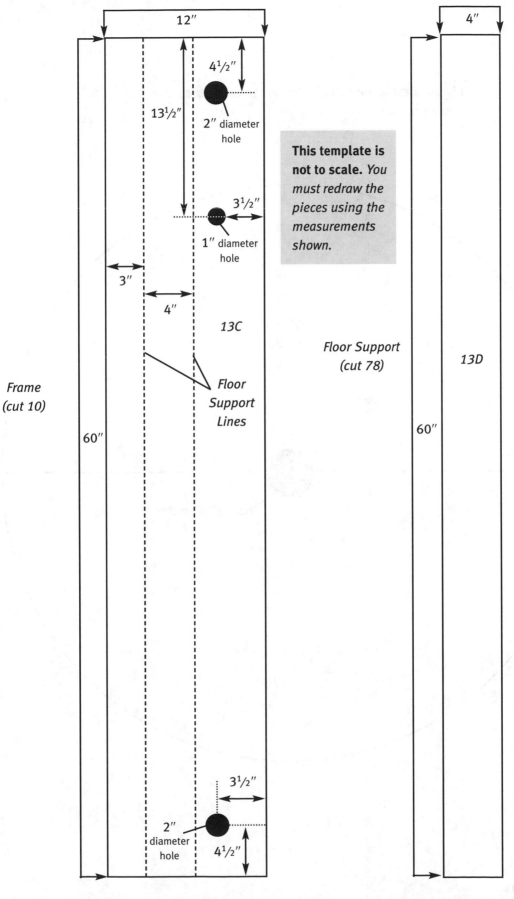

12"

4 1/2"

2" diameter
hole

13 1/2"

3 1/2"

1" diameter
hole

3"

4"

**This template is
not to scale.** *You
must redraw the
pieces using the
measurements
shown.*

13C

*Floor
Support
Lines*

*Floor Support
(cut 78)*

13D

*Frame
(cut 10)*

60"

60"

3 1/2"

2"
diameter
hole

4 1/2"

4"

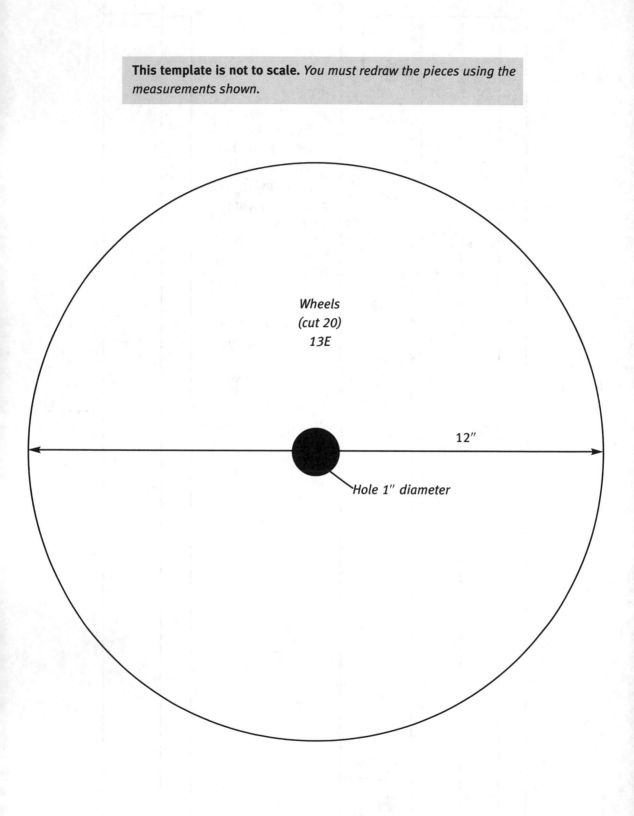

Wheels
(cut 20)
13E

12"

Hole 1" diameter

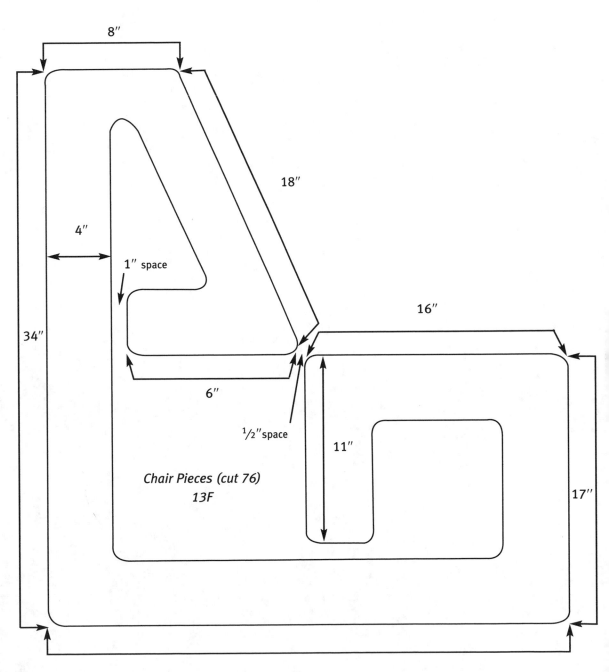

8″

18″

4″

1″ space

34″

6″

16″

½″ space

11″

17″

Chair Pieces (cut 76)
13F

32″

Also Available from Chicago Review Press

Gonzo Gizmos

Projects & Devices to Channel Your Inner Geek

By Simon Field

1556525206
$16.95 (CAN $25.95)

"Recommended."
—*Science News*

"Ideal for science teachers who are looking for new ways to hold their students' interest."
—*Library Journal*

The Art of the Catapult

Build Greek Ballistae, Roman Onagers, English Trebuchets, and More Ancient Artillery

By William Gurstelle

1556525265
$16.95 (CAN $22.95)

"A fascinating look at world history, military strategy, and physics, related with an engaging yet lighthearted touch."
—*School Library Journal*

"This book is a hoot . . . the modern version of *Fun for Boys* and *Harper's Electricity for Boys*."
—*Natural History*

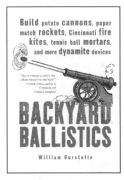

Backyard Ballistics

Build Potato Cannons, Paper Match Rockets, Cincinnati Fire Kites, Tennis Ball Mortars, and More Dynamite Devices

By William Gurstelle

1556523750
$16.95 (CAN $25.95)

"Would-be rocketeers, take note: engineer William Gurstelle has written a book for you."
—*Chicago Tribune*

"Inviting amateur scientists to investigate physics concepts, this book shows how to construct an array of devices exploding with fun."
—*Science News*

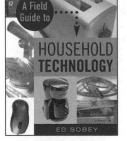

A Field Guide to Household Technology

By Ed Sobey

9781556526701
$14.95 (CAN 18.95)

Illustrating how a fire alarm detects smoke and what the "plasma" is in a plasma screen television, this fascinating handbook explains how more than 180 everyday household devices function and operate.

CHICAGO REVIEW PRESS

Distributed by
Independent Publishers Group
www.ipgbook.com

www.chicagoreviewpress.com